CHURCH TIMES BOOK *of the*
G·A·R·D·E·N

Arnold Currall
and Anne Tubbs

Illustrated by Wendy Bramall

CANTERBURY
PRESS
Norwich

To our gardening friends and especially J.W.

First published in 1997 by The Canterbury Press Norwich
(a publishing imprint of Hymns Ancient & Modern Limited
a registered charity)
St Mary's Works, St Mary's Plain
Norwich, Norfolk, NR3 3BH

British Library Cataloguing in Publication Data

A catalogue record for this book is available from the British Library

ISBN 1-85311-183-X

Typeset by David Gregson Associates, Beccles, Suffolk
Printed in Great Britain by Biddles Ltd, Guildford and King's Lynn

Contents

Acknowledgements

The first named author thanks his host of gardening friends with whom he has spent many hours discussing matters horticultural and to whom he owes much. In particular, he is grateful to the Very Revd Henry Stapleton, Dean of Carlisle, who introduced him to the editor of the *Church Times*, to Sue Maughan for deciphering his handwriting, to David Aitchinson for facsimile facilities, but especially he thanks his wife, Sheila, for reading the original manuscripts and patiently improving their quality, and for her encouragement throughout.

Thanks are also due to Christine Smith of the Canterbury Press who proposed this book and Lesley Walmsley for bringing disparate pieces into one whole. Both authors thank Wendy Bramall for her excellent illustrations which do so much to enhance the appearance of the work.

Introduction

How to cultivate green fingers

Recently a friend asked how I became interested in gardening, and what influences had been significant. The environment in which a child is brought up can be a major influence, and in my case my father and my grandfather were keen amateur gardeners. Both kept their respective households supplied with fresh vegetables and potatoes through most of the year, as well as having very colourful flower displays from spring to autumn. Like most small children, I was keen to help, and my parents encouraged me by giving me small tasks to do, like picking up the clippings after the lawn edges had been cut, or sweeping the paths.

My grandfather's garden had the added attraction of a large greenhouse, heated by a hand-fired coke boiler, and there he cultivated what seemed to a small boy to be hundreds of boxes of bedding plants, prize tuberous begonias, and tomatoes. It was a joy to hold my grandfather's hand and be taken round his large garden, while he patiently answered my questions: this sort of response to a child does more to encourage interest than almost anything else. My sister and I were also each given a small plot of our own; we dug them, raked them, and then sowed annual flower seeds. The excitement of watching the germination, and

I

then of learning to distinguish flowers from weeds, was all good education.

Another significant influence was the Dig for Victory campaign after the outbreak of war in 1939. From the long, hot summer of 1940 until I joined up in 1942, I worked all my school holidays at a small local nursery which had gone over totally to food production. The recent TV series *The Wartime Garden* reminded me of those days, for the foreman, a man in his 50s, had been trained in a walled garden, and had been in service all his life. Working with him was an education in itself, and he was very patient with my persistent questions.

Three of us worked the nursery/market garden: the younger brother of the owner, the foreman and myself. We also had occasional help from a couple of Land Girls and an old pensioner who helped out with the hoeing in summer. Apart from a very heavy rototiller, there were no mechanical appliances, and everything was done by hand.

Of the four large glasshouses, three were given over entirely to tomatoes and one to cucumbers. There was also a fairly large lean-to glasshouse, a sterilizing unit, and the potting shed which was used for producing flowering pot plants, principally cyclamen, primulas and cinerarias. Outside we grew potatoes, peas, beans, onions, carrots, cabbage in variety, and Brussels sprouts, which all went direct to local shops, whereas the glasshouse crops could also be bought from the house.

The indoor work differed from holiday to holiday. During the summer we tended the tomatoes and cucumbers. The tomatoes were picked early in the morning and sent up to the house for grading by the boss. We then watered, and once a week we removed the side shoots, a filthy job which left one's hands stained black with juice. Again once a week, we gave the plants a feed. Three main fertilizers were used in rotation: a liquid home-brew prepared from sheep-droppings; a proprietary liquid feed; and a granular fertilizer, usually fishmeal-based.

After these food crops were cleared, chrysanthemums were moved in. They received similar feeding, plus a weekly dose of water thoroughly impregnated with soot, which made the foliage bitter, and so discouraged the leafmining maggot which so disfigures the leaves.

At Easter the main task was preparing literally tons of compost to the foreman's own formula, very similar to the John Innes composts of the last half-century. This was needed for the hundreds of boxes of bedding and tomato plants we sold, as well as for the 2,000 or more tomato plants grown in the nursery glasshouses. Pricking out bedding plants is a tedious job, but we got it down to a fine art: after a while I could prick out a box of 50 plants in five minutes, a speed I can still achieve. Today most of this work is done by machine in specialist nurseries.

I gained additional practical experience in the autumn of 1940 by taking the tenancy of a standard-size allotment, 30 yards by 10 yards, in a field set aside for the purpose about a mile from my home. My father bought me a stainless-steel spade and fork – I use them still. It was hard work getting it into shape, but the fertile meadow soil, full of humus, produced wonderful crops. My mother paid me retail prices for all the produce I grew, so I could run it profitably, pay the rent, buy tools (most of which I still have), seeds, fertilizers and insecticides, and still have something for buying the books which formed the basis of my horticultural library.

This period of two to three years of holiday working and culti-vating a full-sized allotment made me decide to become either a market gardener or a nurseryman after demobilization; but, as so often happens, things did not turn out as planned, and I became a geologist instead. Had I stuck to my original plan, I suppose I could have been in at the beginning of the development of profitable garden centres; instead, I developed a lifelong interest in gardening and plants, without any commercial pressures.

Interest in gardening has grown with increased leisure time; 25 per cent of the population now lists gardening as a leisure activity, and this percentage increases annually. Early encouragement, of the kind I received from my family, is boosted for today's children by instruction given in primary schools; and I confidently expect that by the turn of the century, the British, instead of being a nation of shopkeepers, will be a nation of gardeners.

January

Be not afraid of going slowly, be only afraid of standing still.

The extremes of climatic conditions we seem to suffer have set me thinking about climatic change. I tend to regard statements like 'the worst since records began' as alarmist; so I've been doing some research into the writings of the Rev. Gilbert White, the 18th-century naturalist who was curate of Selborne, Hampshire, for 42 years, until his death in 1793. White recorded the changing seasons over this period, together with a virtual day-by-day record of barometer and thermometer readings, and wind directions. From even a cursory study, I gained the impression that the seasons varied then from year to year, much as they do now, in terms of rainfall, temperatures and gales.

White's writings are in roughly four sections, of which two particularly note the weather. *The Garden Kalendar* (1751–67) is a diary of what he and his gardeners were doing. For example, in January 1754 he records 'an uncommon severe winter: most things in the garden destroyed'.

The Naturalists' Journal runs from 1768 until his death, and it is here that the most detailed accounts of weather recordings are to be found, with brief notes on gardening work, farm work, and the arrival and departure of swallows and martins.

Since White's day, it has been difficult to find such detailed accounts of the day-to-day work in the garden. However, I am grateful to Bill Burroughs for an article in *The Garden*, the journal

7

of the Royal Horticultural Society, called 'Forecasting the Future'. He has gathered together in graphic form the rainfall and temperature records for the periods 1765–1995 and 1700–1995 respectively, each year divided into the winter half (October to March) and the growing season (April to September).

The results do not really support the dire predictions. There has been a steady increase in the average winter rainfall over the 230-year period, from 450mm to 530mm, but this is roughly balanced by a drop in the summer rainfall. The summer average temperature has remained at about 13.1C over 295 years, but the winter average temperature has risen from 5C to 5.9C.

A careful study of the diagrams shows no evidence of changing conditions, only the usual variations on a yearly basis. If we are considering new plants to grow, we will be wise to include a high proportion of hardy but drought-resistant species, while at the same time improving the drainage and the condition of the soil to produce flourishing flowers and vegetables.

Visiting gardens

A spare morning during a visit to Oxford gave me the opportunity of renewing my acquaintance with the University Botanical Gardens, the oldest botanical gardens in England, and among the first in Europe. Their form is very much as originally arranged in the 17th century, with the main beds containing members of one family or genus. Since the gardens owe their origins to medicine and teaching, and are still a major resource for teaching and research in the plant world, the taxonomic (or biologically classified) arrangement is suitable for their purpose and shows that there is more than one way of presenting information.

The gardens face south and occupy a relatively sheltered spot beside the River Cherwell at Magdalen Bridge; a good part is bounded by high stone walls of warm Cotswold stone of the Jurassic period. It was interesting to note what differences a sheltered site and a latitudinal distance of about 200 miles from my own garden make to the growth and flowering of some plants.

For example, there were snowdrops in full flower, and nearby the lovely white rose *Rosa chinensis* was still in bloom, along with the white, scented honeysuckle *Lonicera purpusii*.

During my visit I saw only about a dozen other people, and I was surprised by the apparent absence of staff in the gardens. I couldn't help wondering whether they are affected by theft, as are many of the gardens open to the public under the National Gardens Scheme and on other charitable occasions. All too often whole plants are dug up and removed, and I can only assume that it is experts who do this, since it is obvious that they know exactly what to take. Even on my last visit to Wisley I saw a woman starting to dig up a plant on the rockery. It is my experience that the people who open their gardens are only too willing to talk about their plants, and not infrequently offer a seedling or a cutting without even being asked.

The flower garden

Walking round the garden, I find some signs of unseasonable growth, especially under shrubs and bushes. Under the *Philadelphus coronaria*, snowdrops are about three inches high, their buds almost showing white. Part of the pulmonaria Sissinghurst White, which has spread under the shelter of a small specimen of *Choisya ternata*, is blooming, although the main part of the clump is obviously dormant. Some years ago I planted a relation of the English elm, *Zelkova serrata*, which is native to

9

China, Korea and Japan, and which in due course will be a medium-sized tree: around its base, daffodils are already two to three inches high.

I have noticed that bulbs and plants round trees and shrubs do tend to start into growth sooner than those further away. I'm not certain that this is always because of the shelter they offer; it seems to me that the soil in the area round trees may well be warmer than that further away. Thaw of snow or frost tends to move outwards from tree trunks. I don't know if this is the result of some physiological activity in the tree roots, or because of a drier soil, or whether there is some quite other cause.

The kitchen garden

The next job in the vegetable plot must be to plant the garlic cloves, for garlic enjoys a long growing season and if planted now, about four inches deep, will show its first leaves in about ten weeks' time. Like most members of the onion family, garlic likes a deep, highly fertile soil, and I find it does best if grown on the same plot each year, along with shallots and onions.

As soon as I can get on the ground with the aid of boards, I will plant not only the garlic but also the shallots: as with the garlic, I save the best shallot bulbs, both red and yellow, each year. Covering them with cloches or fleece will help to warm the soil and start them into growth, and will also stop the birds disturbing them before they are properly rooted.

I'm sure I'm not alone in finding difficulty in tying onions in strings to hang up for storage, in the way of the Breton or Spanish onion-sellers. My wife and I have found an easier way, which also ensures them an adequate circulation of air. We simply take discarded stockings or tights, and drop the onions one by one down the leg, tying a knot between each onion. By cutting a slit in the stocking, each onion can be taken out as desired. Should one onion rot, it will not contaminate its neighbour because no two onions touch each other. Our woodshed is now festooned with different-coloured stockings full of onions, hanging from nails in the beams.

General tasks

As soon as the weather warms up a little and the snow disappears, I will complete the winter pruning of the fruit. The cordon apples need to have this year's growth further shortened to three buds, as do the fan-trained Victoria plum, the greengage, and the red- and whitecurrants, to encourage the development of good fruiting buds. A number of new shoots on the currants will provide ideal cuttings for rooting to give replacement plants in a year's time.

We often forget that many plants will just not go on for ever, and then wonder why they begin to look sickly and do not fruit as well. Apart from the problems of overcrowding as clumps grow, the main reason for dividing up herbaceous plants by separating off new healthy shoots for propagation is to maintain strong and vigorous plants. Soft-fruit plants likewise become tired after a few years, lose their vigour, and become more susceptible to disease. Strawberries certainly need replacing regularly, and some commercial growers do this every year. I find replacing every three years is best, on the basis that the first year gives the largest fruit, the second year the heaviest crop, and the third year a good crop for jam-making.

Gooseberry and red- and whitecurrant bushes or cordons last longer than this – mine are now 12 years old, but are not producing as heavily as they did and so will be replaced either this spring or next. Raspberries are so susceptible to disease that I find I am lucky to get more than five years' fruiting from them.

Although there is little to be done outside just now, it is worth checking that all plants needing some winter protection are satisfactorily covered.

Flower for the month: *Helleborus Niger* – Christmas Rose

We are told that these white, chalice-shaped flowers grew in Paradise, where the angels called them roses of love. After the Fall, when snow fell in Paradise and many flowers suffered, the roses of love remained immaculate in the snow, so when the angels heard of the birth of a baby King in mid-winter, they asked God's permission to take these plants to earth to adorn the stable. Many medieval paintings of the Nativity include Christmas roses, and perhaps we should add them to our Christmas scenes.

Flowers for the house

Cut branches of flowering shrubs, such as flowering currant, forsythia and *spiraea arguta*, and leave in water in a cool place for a succession of early flowers. Flowering currant bloom will be snow-white without a trace of unpleasant smell.

The scent of hyacinths in pots can be overpowering. Sometimes it is worth cutting one or two to put in a small vase with a few leaves.

In the cold of January it is easy to raise room temperature to the discomfort of house plants, or to damage Christmas plant gifts with overwatering. Be sparing.

Flowers for the church

Most churches are so cold that the white flowers used for Christmas decoration will still be in a state of chilled perfection at Epiphany, which is a financial relief in an expensive month. Probably there will be white carnations, which, with their coloured sisters, are addicted to fizzy lemonade. It is an economy to indulge them and extend their life considerably. Chrysanthemum blooms also survive for several weeks in undisturbed splendour. There is still plenty of greenery about, and ivy should still be flowering.

I have never seen pot plants used in church decoration, but in America banked up pots of poinsettias are not unusual. In a parish where the local mayor worships, and has contacts with the borough parks and gardens, this might be worth trying, with great discretion.

The children's garden – *Creating a garden for birds*

Gardeners are not all bent old men: many are young enough to have adventures. Find out about the journeys of John Tradescant, and his son, John, who collected plants from all over the world in the 16th century.

If you are a young gardener it is important not to be overfaced by too large a plan; a small area round a bird-table could be fun. A shrub, pyracantha or cotoneaster, with flowers, and later on berries, and a container of water, would please the birds. You could grow a water-loving plant in this, with a few spring bulbs or primulas nearby. Crocuses are not a good idea as the birds might eat them. If it is possible to collect a few big stones, these would hold pockets of earth in which to plant rockery pinks or saxifrage or, later on, trailing lobelia, which flower for a long time. Enjoy experimenting.

Things to enjoy

- The wonderful light and shadow on snow, but remember its weight: sustainable by a frail snowdrop, but a damaging calamity for hedges and shrubs. Knock it off gently.

- A few minutes' extra daylight in the mornings and evenings, and the first loosening of winter's grip. The first hesitant bird song. Late Christmas roses and early aconites and snowdrops.

- The full range of root vegetables available, in the greengrocer's, if not in your garden. An invitation to cold weather soups and stews.

February

All gardeners know better than other gardeners.

The beauty of February, the last month of winter proper, lies not so much in the promise of spring but in February's own inimitable character. It is the month of design, and perspective without the barrier of trees in full foliage, or the distraction of nearer plant growth. It is pleasing to imagine that this might have been Capability Brown's favourite month; a time when his elegant landscaping could be appreciated in all its restrained perfection. Our vicarage garden, through no effort of ours, fits exactly into the distant view: in front of the house grass enclosed by clipped privet; steps down to the kitchen garden, sloping down to the beck, with hazels, hollies, sycamores and yews along the bank; rising across the glebe field to a great old ash tree; across another field, the cricket ground, and on through the National Park up to the Nabs, the escarpment on the skyline. The bare branches of nearer trees break this line with their stark silhouettes, and against a dull gold sunset, with a line of silver birches on one wing and the headstones in the churchyard on the other, you have a stage set needing no actors. It is easy to agree with John Buchan: 'It is the English winter that intoxicates me, more even than the English May, for the noble bones of the land are bare, and you get the essential savour of earth and wood and water.'

You also get the Fair Maids of February, the glory of the month. One or other variety of galanthus is usually in flower from mid-

January throughout February, white drifts all over the churchyard, cascading down the beck banks and clustered in all the village gardens, blooming more sparsely under the trees like drops shaken from some vast celestial milk jug. A discussion with a friend on new varieties of snowdrop ended with advice to search in a certain row of gardens for a new variety, whose pure white petals are reversed with flat, dark green. Even gardeners can have their legs pulled, though it took some time to realize that only lunatics pursue their way invading the edges of their neighbours' gardens, lifting all the snowdrop bells, hoping to discover green linings.

One adverse quirk of fate which strikes gardeners at this time of year is the second helping of leaves. Sweep them up in early winter as thoroughly as may be, more will inevitably appear when the snow melts; and unless timing is perfect one sits uncomfortably on the horns of a dilemma: sweep them up, and damage new growth and behead the snowdrops: or leave them, and new growth is clogged and the garden untidy.

February is not a month one would normally associate with perfume, but as the sun gains some power the scent of wallflowers is noticeable; Cherry Pie flowers, winter heliotrope, are sending waves of perfume across the road. Strongest of all is the hauntingly aromatic smell from the replenished log pile, a small mountain of huge trunk sections from what must have been a Goliath of a cypress tree. Suddenly obtrusive every year is the unmistakable, but unidentifiable, smell of spring, which accompanies an urgent sense that the natural world is stirring. It is the season to recall, with gentle enjoyment, a cleric who thoroughly aroused all the garden enthusiasts in his congregation on Sexagesima. His eloquence on the fall of man, and holy horticulture, tosticated his congregation, by an erudite route through the garden of Eden –

surely his text must have been 'the story of man began in a garden – and ended in Revelation'. Could it be that he included the Countess von Arnim's down-to-earth diary entry in 1898: 'It is not graceful, and it makes one hot, but it is a blessed sort of work, and if Eve had had a spade in Paradise, and known how to use it, we should not have had all that sad business of the apple.'

Rain and wind

Rain, snow, gales and frequently severe frosts are guaranteed for February, so it is hard to believe that there will be any water shortage for a very long time to come. The snow and ice are really little more than a temporary nuisance, but excessive rain, and the gales can have more serious consequences. There is frequently a lot of flooding and the gardens become sodden, so that no outside work is possible.

In the gales of 1993 the stays securing my damson tree snapped, and since the soil was in a semi-plastic condition the trunk took on a somewhat drunken look, at an angle of 45 degrees. I thought my Brussels sprouts, curly kale and purple sprouting broccoli were secure, being planted deep and earthed up, but now most of them are lying flat and a few were actually blown out of the ground.

The flower garden

In spite of the weather, it is a joy to wander round the garden and see the first signs of spring flowers. *Viburnum x bodnantense* has been blooming since early December, but around its base the first snowdrops are now flowering; and nearby are the pale-yellow *Hamamelis mollis* var. Pallida, and the dark copper-red

H. x intermedia var. Diane, all looking slightly incongruous against the snowy backcloth. *Sycopsis sinensis*, related to hamamelis, is also in bloom: a plant not often seen, it is a very useful slow-growing evergreen flowering shrub. *Lonicera x purpusii*, planted against the rear wall of the house 18 months ago, is flowering this year for the first time. A woody member of the honeysuckle family, it is certainly a bonus for the early months of the year, with its sweet-smelling white flowers. It does well, pruned fairly hard back, as a wall shrub facing the south or south-west.

The spring bulbs make me feel much more cheerful. The winter aconites, *Eranthis hyemalis*, are looking quite stately, with the ring of bright green leaves forming a ruff immediately below the flowers. Snowdrops and aconites mix well, and look particularly attractive round the trunks of trees or round deciduous shrubs. In sheltered places the crocuses are already making a splash of colour in their shades of blue and yellow. On the edge of my rock garden is a patch of species type crocus which we acquired a few years ago from the derelict garden of an empty farmhouse. It is a very pale blue, and I do not know its name or variety, but it is always the earliest to flower.

The greenhouse and cold frame

One of the best and longest-lasting flowering pot plants for the house, provided the atmosphere is not too dry, is the florist's azalea, *A. indica*. They flower from about Christmas through until Easter, and grow best in a crock pot, requiring little attention apart from adequate moisture and an occasional feed. When flowering is over, I move them into a frost-free place to harden off until late April or May, when they are plunged into an outdoor bed until about September. Any pruning is done after flowering, and, if necessary, the plants can be repotted at the same time.

The other plant making a colourful show at the present time is *Primula malacoides*, a dainty and very free-flowering plant, in shades of pink, pale mauve, pale brick-red and white, sometimes known as the Fairy Primrose. I am not aware that handling it leads to any skin problems. Although *P. malacoides* can be grown as a short-lived perennial, I prefer to treat it as an annual and grow it each year from seed.

Once I bought an old pot-bound orchid, a cymbidium without a label, for £1 from a plant stall at a fundraising event for the church. I've always thought it would be fun to grow orchids, if only for the feeling of one-up-manship that it gives; and I was encouraged by one of my books which said: 'Cymbidiums are generally easy to grow, require cool conditions, and are ideal for newcomers to orchid culture.' Late in the spring I divided the old plant into about ten pieces, making sure that each contained a growing pseudobulb, and after potting them up in orchid compost, I placed them in a relatively shaded part of the glasshouse. What a thrill it was the following February to find that one of them had grown a long flower stalk and the first buds were breaking into bloom.

Last spring I was given a few pseudobulbs of two other 'easy' orchids, which I brought into growth on a window ledge in the spare bedroom, near a night-storage heater. I am delighted to report that one of them, *Dendrobium kingianum*, which originates in Queensland, Australia, is just coming into bloom.

Flower for the month: *Galanthus Nivalis* – Snowdrop

At the beginning of February, the coldest, darkest part of the year, the Church celebrates Candlemas, the great festival of light, in honour of the Purification of the Blessed Virgin Mary. At the same time, nature in both parallel and association rejoices in the first snowdrops; Persephone returns from the underworld. A great Gothic cathedral with no light except two altar candles is an eerie place until the light is passed from person to person and the whole congregation processes with the clergy in a blaze of singing and light. No less dramatic are the tiny white flames of the first snow-drops, 'Fair Maids of February', pushing through the dark earth, or even bearing a weight of snow. Also known as Candlemas Bells and Mary's Tapers, in the Welsh border country a bowl of snowdrops brought indoors was believed to confer the 'white purification'.

As there are few references to snowdrops by early garden writers, it was assumed that they were late comers to this country, but this is probably because they were formerly known as bulbous violets. Certainly by 1465 they were in use as an effective emmenogogue and their strong Church association is probably much older still.

Flowers for the house

This is the time to enjoy your own home-grown spring flowers. If, however, you lack space, warmth or enthusiasm, then living decoration for February becomes something of a challenge. For a large space the bare red stems of dogwood, with just a few glossy dark leaves, look well where sunshine can light them. Snowdrops, bunched with ivy leaves, are unoriginal, but light up beautifully against dark wood; dark green pernettya has the brightest pink berries – it also has prickles, so be careful, and there are several varieties of viburnum in sweet-scented bloom.

Flowers for the church

If Easter falls early, much of February will fall in Lent, when there will be no flowers in church. This is an agreeable break, but also a good time to spring-clean all containers; throw away old oasis and order a fresh supply; and if Easter is late, pray for a wedding or two to help out with flowers at the expensive time before Lent. Early daffodils and iris seem an obvious choice, but can be difficult to handle if they are weak in the stem, or may never really warm up.

The children's garden – *A patch of colour*

If you have a plot of earth with which you may do as you like, what about collecting cast-offs and self-seeds, which cost nothing?

Gardeners divide all sorts of perennial plants in February, and throw away the surplus. Ask if you may have spare roots. Dig your patch; break up the lumps and rake over, then plant according to expected size. Many plants, such as forget-me-nots, set their own seed, often where they are not wanted. Look for seedlings and ask if you may transplant them. Nothing could be prettier than an edging of alternating daisies and dandelions, usefully weeded from the lawn, but do be careful to cut the dead heads or they will spread everywhere.

Things to enjoy

- The smell of winter heliotrope, if you can find some.

- Golden falls of winter jasmine; shy patches of pale starry *anemone blanda*; and floods of snowdrops.

- Browsing through nurserymen's spring catalogues.

- Sowing some flower and vegetable seeds indoors, so long as you have adequate shelter for the resulting seedlings.

- Visiting herbaceous plants to check for signs of life after the winter.

- St Valentine's Day, 14 February, the birds' wedding day.

March

He who plants a garden, plants happiness.

March is generally called the first month of spring. Writers of the 'hey-nonny-no' school have obviously never sat out in March, or early April, on the north-east coast. Any 'pretty country folk' dallying on the grass can expect severe hypothermia; while any housewife reckless enough to hang out her washing anticipating 'the soft wing of vernal breeze to be shed' on it, would probably be obliged to collect her laundry from our neighbours in Holland. However, the vexations of life tend to level out, and though it may be tantalizing near chilly Scarborough to brood on thoughts of flowers already displaying in the milder south-west, at least we are spared the horror of hordes of snails which, we are told, climb up posting boxes at this time of year, to munch through nutritious collections of letters, attracted by the alluring smell of human saliva on stamps and envelope flaps. Dare the Royal Mail offer this as an excuse for raising postal charges? It seems all too reminiscent of British Rail's trains' inability to cope with leaves on the lines.

It is an interesting parallel that the spiritual endeavours of the long penitential season of Lent coincide with the gardener's laborious preparation for the season of new growth in the garden, and that the reward of both disciplines begins at Easter, or thereabouts, reflecting in both cases the persistence of the groundwork: and groundwork it is at this time of year – with a spade.

Admirable the person who has the strength, and resolution, to begin digging and continue until it is completed. It may be an excuse for personal frailty, but I suspect that Adam's back is more competently designed for turning the earth than Eve's. Certainly one Eve avoids muscle strain with frequent changes of jobs – tying up, hand weeding, moving useful self-seeds to a holding bed, and so on; but what a relief to be ambidextrous.

Browse in any bookshop and it would seem that the English are chiefly occupied in their kitchens and gardens. Of course the two go hand in hand, and the old adage that nothing is new is proved by two gardening books published in 1688 and 1726 respectively, in which the layout is exactly the same as in many contemporary publications. Both books contain sections on trees, flowers, fruit, soil structure, and so on, together with month-by-month instructions for work to be done and what flowers should be 'blowing'. Modern books may discuss a wider range of plants, but the 18th-century professor packs an immense amount of diverse information into one compact volume, much of it highly technical as to the control of heat, seed husbandry and the chemistry of soil. The cultivation of such exotica as truffles, guava, coffee, prickly pears, malabar nuts and pomegranates is discussed as casually as though they were as common as daisies, and as easy to grow. Londoners are commended for the beauty of their ranunculus, of which there are too many varieties to mention as 'so many sorts are brought in from Turkey every year'. At a time when the choice of land transport was two legs or four, the labour and risk of plant importing is difficult to imagine.

It must be a sop to British pride that a French gardener, long since dead, allowed that rosemary seed will not germinate in French soil, so that one should beg cuttings from an English friend. This same gardener helpfully advises how to pack these cuttings for successful transportation: 'Wrap them in waxed cloth, sew up the cloth, smear with honey, and powder it well with wheat flour.' What a delicious challenge for HM Customs' sniffer dogs.

Frost and aphids

The severe frosts of February have helped to improve the texture of the soil by opening up the interstices between the grains of sand and silt; and there were also a good number of clear sunny days with drying easterly winds.

Severe winter frosts are useful in another way too: they reduce the population of aphids, flies and other bugs which can cause gardening headaches later in the year. We are, I think, beginning to realize that in many ways the main beneficiaries of insecticides are the manufacturers, since each new insecticide seems to encourage the development of a more resistant strain of insect. One way forward is the breeding of predators that feed on the pests – for example, encasia, which eat whitefly in greenhouses. But I cannot help wondering whether this may itself not contain hidden dangers.

The flower garden

Some warm sun is all that is needed to bring out fully not only any remaining snowdrops but also aconites and crocuses. In addition to the usual blue, yellow and white hybrid crocus, we have species varieties such as *C. sativus*, *C. tommasinianus* and *C. fuscotinctus* which have more delicate flowers and are more softly coloured. They made a cheerful sight, and are a hopeful sign that spring is not far away.

Many shrubs also start showing buds, if not actual colour. Those of the rhododendrons swell noticeably in March, even though most of them will not flower until late April or May. *Viburnum juddii*, the compact and highly scented variety, is a mass of buds, and I look forward, at about Easter-tide, to a fine show from it, and also from *Osmanthus delavayi*. I am delighted to see that the first leaves and flowers are appearing on the dogtooth violets (*Erythronium dens canis*). It is not always easy to get established; once it is, it resents disturbance.

After snow the garden has a somewhat bedraggled air. However, the stalks and dead foliage of last year's herbaceous perennials do provide protection from the worst effects of snow and frost, even for plants regarded as only semi-hardy or even tender; and although I always dig up clumps of *Lobelia cardinalis* and the named pentstemons to keep in a frost-free place over winter, those left in the ground invariably seem to survive. In a sheltered spot at the back of the house *Cyclamen trochopteranthum* is in full bloom: a native of south-west Turkey, it is good to know that it has survived its first years outdoors. It was a great pleasure to find not only *Helleborus atrorubens* a mass of lovely wine-red flowers, fully out, but also *H. niger*, of which I had despaired at Christmas. The two clumps are side by side, in a sheltered spot, beneath a tall *Cotoneaster franchettii* which also plays host to the Japanese honeysuckle *Aureoreticulata*, which has attractive yellow-veined leaves.

The pulmonaria are showing a variety of colour which certainly compensates for their rather dull, messy appearance through most of the summer. A number of varieties are worthwhile growing, apart from *P. officinalis*. In recent years I have added *P. rubra* var. Bowles Red, which has salmon-red flowers and is one of the earliest to bloom; and also *P. angustifolia* var.

Munstead Blue, which retains its deep blue colour until it finishes flowering and ultimately dies right down. Last year I acquired the striking *P. officinalis* var. Sissinghurst White. It is useful to have a white flower in spring, other than snowdrops.

The kitchen garden

I have also been able to weed and dig over the whole of the fruit-cage area, and to weed most of the remainder of the kitchen garden before digging. Regular weeding is much cheaper than chemical weedkillers, assuming that the labour is 'free'; and unless the weeds are in seed, or are pernicious creeping perennials like nettle, convolvulus or ground elder (called bishop's weed, in this area) they provide good material for the compost heap. Two large bins of compost, together with the contents of last year's growbags, used for tomatoes and cucumbers, are now waiting to be dug in.

There are not many vegetables left in the kitchen garden, except leeks, but the Brussels sprouts have done well – we had the final picking for lunch just before Lent – and the cabbage patch is now virtually cleared. The onions have kept well this winter, and we will certainly have enough for us until Easter, at least.

I have a certain amount of club root in the garden, but this problematic disease of the cabbage family has not really affected either the quality or the quantity of the crops. Though much conflicting advice is given about the disease, I have concluded that there is no really effective remedy. It tends to be worst on heavy, acid soils, and a dressing of lime at digging time may help to keep it in check. Many authors recommend crop rotation, but most amateur gardeners have small gardens and so this may not be possible. I have found that the disease can be reasonably well contained by raising each plant in a three- or four-inch pot filled with a proprietary potting mixture or a sterilized soil compost, and then planting out the whole soil ball as well as the young plant. Club root is rare in field-grown brassicas.

The seed potatoes are now set out in egg trays in the spare bedroom to 'chit'. Good Friday is traditionally the day for planting the first earlies outside – that might be feasible if the date of Easter were fixed towards the end of April, but whenever I have tried planting potatoes on Good Friday they have invariably been cut down by frost, or else have been attacked later on by slugs or wireworms. Besides a few of the salad variety, Pink Fir Apple, I am growing only the early varieties Arran Pilot and Home Guard. I will grow some of them on in pots, and then plant them in a plastic dustbin with holes bored in the base for drainage. This makes it possible to have a succession of early potatoes until the autumn.

Another job has been to prune back the gooseberries and redcurrants to one bud on all the new growth. This, by reducing the number of fruiting buds, will encourage big, well formed fruit, and in the case of the gooseberries will certainly make picking the fruit easier later in the year.

The greenhouse and cold frame

Even if there is little that can be done outside, there is plenty of inside work. One of my frequent new-year resolutions is to wash all pots, boxes and labels thoroughly after use and store them ready for reuse. It is inconvenient, to say the least, to find that there are no clean pots of the right size when repotting, and no clean labels either; and the washing (add a little Jeyes Fluid to the water) helps improve hygiene in the greenhouse, even if the kitchen sink does sometimes get clogged up. It also pays to make sure that your supplies of pots, compost, fertilizer, fungicide and insecticide are bought well in advance, not because there might be a shortage, but simply to make sure they are there when needed.

It is noticeable that the non-soil-based composts – peat, coir, and so on – give very little specific information on their labels: the John Innes formulae, set up about 60 years ago, aimed at providing just this information and standardization, so that it is possible to add more of some ingredients, such as peat for lime-hating plants like heathers, or coarse sand or grit for pinks and carnations. I certainly use soil-less, so-called multi-purpose, composts, mainly for pricking out seedlings of bedding plants, but I would like to have more details about their formulae.

We are always being told never to use composts more than once, because they may contain disease spores, or may be exhausted. Last summer I potted up seedlings of five or six differ-ent species of cyclamen. The gritty seed mixture in which they germinated was just what I needed to add to some soil-less compost to make it more open-textured for potting on other plants, so I used it – and was a little surprised last week to find cyclamen seedlings emerging in the pots of various greenhouse plants. Although I don't yet know which of the species of cycla-men these are, it shows that sometimes we can get away with breaking the rules.

There have been some delightful new varieties of hyacinths on the market in the last few years. Gypsy Queen (a vibrant salmon-pink) and Sky Jacket (a clear pale blue) are two outstanding vari-eties; they have done exceptionally well, making good strong growth and eight-inch stems of tightly bunched flowers. I can thoroughly recommend both these varieties. As the bulbs finish flowering, I reduce the watering, and after about a fortnight knock the bulbs out of the pots, laying them carefully on their sides in the greenhouse to dry off and ripen, before planting them outside in the autumn.

Heavy rain, bitter east winds, and quantities of snow often continue into March, yet signs of spring are everywhere. So I am often emboldened in February to start sowing seeds in the greenhouse. The early seeds were germinated in electric propagators which stand on the windowsill of the spare bedroom, because there is no electricity at the greenhouse. The first seeds sown included cauliflower, the variety All the Year Round. The seedlings are now in the greenhouse, and almost ready to be potted up singly, so that about Easter-time they will be planted out, under cloches or under horticultural fleece. They should be ready for cutting in early June.

Red onions are just ready to germinate, and will be planted out in the open ground at the end of April or the beginning of May. For the main onion crop, I am relying on sets of the same three varieties that I have grown for some years: Centurion, Stuttgart and Turbo. Because the ground has been so wet and I like to get both onion sets and shallots started early, I have planted them up

in boxes in the greenhouse. I find it a good idea to take shallots and onion sets out of their packaging, and keep them in a light airy place, because they are very susceptible to mildew.

Some bedding plants benefit from a long growing season. Since they may be needed for hanging baskets and other containers, the petunias and African marigolds have already been sown and are beginning to germinate. In the first week in March the antirrhinums, asters, salpiglossis, nicotiana, nemesia and lobelia were sown; after being pricked out into boxes, they will be hardened off ready for planting out by the middle of May. It is always tempting to sow all the early plants at the same time, but I stagger sowings over a period of a fortnight or so, which ensures that a steady flow of boxes into the greenhouse can be maintained, and an equally steady flow into the frames, to begin the hardening-off process before planting out.

The plants over-wintered in the greenhouse are also starting into growth, and now need a little more water. Both the fuchsias and geraniums are developing growths suitable for taking as cuttings. This is not the best time to take geranium cuttings because they tend to damp off, but watering, once only, with a fungicide mixture after potting will control this. My tuberous begonias are so large that once they have started growth again I will cut them into pieces, each with a growing shoot, and dust them with a fungicide powder to prevent rotting, before potting them up as well. I will also be potting up the little achimenes tubers – this is a good time to start, providing you can maintain a temperature of about 60 degrees Fahrenheit in a propagator.

The trailing fuchsias, geraniums and fibrous-rooted *Begonia semperflorens*, which were the main plantings in the hanging baskets last year, have started to grow in the greenhouse, and in a few weeks' time I will pot them up with a view to using them again – perhaps in the window boxes this time. In the greenhouse, the fritillaria are almost in flower: although they are a genus of hardy bulbs they can be temperamental in this country. They prefer a sunny, well-drained site, but do well in a cool green-house: I have grown *F. acmopetela*, *F. michalovskia* and *F. biflora* Martha Roderick very successfully in pots for the last few years. The bulbs are not cheap to buy, so it pays to take care. *F. meleagis*, the snakeshead fritillary, growing out in the garden, is a native of Great Britain, and I recall seeing whole meadows of these white-and-purple-chequered bell-like flowers many years ago in Berkshire. The Crown Imperial, *F. imperialis*, which is the largest fritillary and perfectly hardy, can be shy to flower, especially if it is not planted deeply enough.

Flower for the month: Narcissus

For most of us it is the members of the huge narcissus family in their cheering shades of cream, gold, white and yellow which assure us that winter is past and the burgeoning growth of spring is again with us. The name belongs to the misty age of myth and legend, before the written word was common and the details of stories told, and retold, became blurred.

One version tells of Narcissus, a beautiful youth, who spurned the love of Echo because he had fallen in love with his own reflection which he gazed at in a pool of clear water: from this we derive our word *narcissism*, self-love. A more attractive variation claims that Narcissus seeing his own reflection thought it was the spirit of his beloved twin sister for whose death he grieved. He spent so much time in mourning beside the water that the gods pitied him and turned him into a flower with its head hanging down so that he could forever gaze into the clear pool.

Flowers for the house

There is usually no shortage of flowers in March, nor of fresh greenery to support them.

For arrangements in large spaces there is the beginning of the flood of flowering trees and shrubs, as well as daffodils and the succeeding narcissi. One of the early flowers is white *amelanchier canadensis*, followed by forsythia (equally effective cut tall, or quite short), and all the varieties of prunus, crataegus and malus, airy clouds of pink and white.

Daffodils may just as successfully be built into a twisting spiral of gold heads rising from a shallow bowl, massed with tall foliage, or supported sparsely in a narrow glass for a small space.

Hazel twigs are perfect to support grape hyacinths, scillas, or early anemones; and primulas informally bunched in a mug are cheerful.

Every garden needs a bergenia plant, both for its shiny flat leaves and the pink flowers which blend with early blossom.

Ahead lies six months' growth to experiment with.

Flowers for the church

Much of this month is likely to pass preparing for Easter, the triumphant pinnacle of the liturgical cycle, when churches celebrate in a blaze of white and gold, both echoing the natural colours of renewal in the spring garden, and in ecstatic contrast to the austerity of Lent and winter.

This is a time of some anxiety. Will daffodils in the churchyard and vicarage garden be flowering, or, if they are past their best, will the narcissi be ready? What if the altar lilies, ordered well in advance, are disappointingly small, or if irises, among the more temperamental of florists' blooms, stage a complete collapse? Or what to do if all the flower arrangers decide to spend Easter abroad, or some generous parishioner brings masses of pink tulips?

The children's garden – *An alpine garden*

If there is very little space in the garden where you live it might still be possible to create an alpine garden in a sunny spot. In the best of all possible worlds you need an old stone drinking trough, but an old sink, shower tray, or any stout container would do. Alpines, whose original home was in rocky, mountain districts, are usually low growing and colourful. They need good drainage and appreciate a layer of fine gravel around their roots. Many of them are spring-flowering, but as gaps occur you could easily fill the containers with a punnet of annuals. Lobelia flowers for a long time, with a few of the trailing variety to hang down the sides.

Tailpiece

There is often concern about the standard of plants on sale at garden centres. The quality certainly does vary, but I find the majority of centres maintain an acceptable standard. The few poor or bad centres tend to look untidy, and the pots or boxes have plenty of weeds along with the plant for sale, which suggests that it has been on the shelf too long.

If a plant looks sad, it is suffering from stress – either from lack, or excess, of moisture; from too much sun, or from too much shade. A stressed plant will not thrive. Plants, like domestic animals, respond to love and attention; so among all the other care you give your plants I suggest talking to them. They know then that they are wanted. My wife says this is all nonsense, and that it is just my excuse for talking to myself. All I can say is that, in my experience, the plants respond – and I feel better.

Things to enjoy

- The scent of new-mown grass if the weather is suitable for a first cut.

- The first silver sheen of whitebeam leaves.

- Looking out for clumps of primroses, cowslips and violets, in your gardens or in hedgerows.

- Small patches of colour in the garden, expanding into isolated pools: primulas, forget-me-nots, pansies all stirring.

- Early lambs decorating the fields.

April

The man who cannot take his eyes from his magnolias
has no seduction for women.

Gardening in April is rather like going to a party. There are the familiar friends and neighbours to greet, those whose accepted presence give quiet contentment – flowering shrubs and spring bulbs who are always welcome. Then there are new residents to meet, like the species tulip *Turkestanica*, whose demure cream flowers make a well-dressed edging – 'Hello, have you really come from Asia Minor?' Another bright little newcomer, *Pachysandra*, is mingling well, spreading itself and already over-powering its neighbours. Further away stands an ostentatious, over-perfumed group of naturalizing hyacinths in purple, pink and white – 'Why, I saw you last year in pots on a London balcony.' Every good party has gate-crashers, and here we have a family of red orach, more acceptable to the eye than the palate. Finally one must check on the health of late arrivals – 'How are the dog violets?' 'Rather late, I'm afraid; the lilies look fragile, but the hostas are becoming ebullient guests.'

As the days get longer the competition for choir-bird-of-the-year begins at first light, with the exuberant shrieks and clapping wings of a cock pheasant. Every year gulls scream challenges from our neighbours' roof, taken up by the morbidly raucous cacophony from the pair of carrion crows which always nest in the vicarage fir tree; a newly established rookery adds to the clamour, while the piping descant of the songbirds soars over all. Only the ageing village peacock lies late in bed.

Some years ago it seemed a good idea to grow amaryllis bulbs as Christmas presents; they leapt into such surging growth that it was difficult to find anywhere cool enough to slow them down. Practice does not always make perfect: the following year I grew white ones called Christmas Gift, which grew so sluggishly that they were not blooming until Easter – handsome, eventually, but stodgy, hardly 'Amaryllis dancing in green'.

This month there would be sufficient movement in the herb patch to be useful; the first bright frills of parsley, enough chives to cheer up the cheese in a sandwich, enough mint for sauce to accompany Easter lamb, if the cook remembers to pick it; and trust the dandelions not to be backward, but they do add bite to early salad, or chopped over potatoes. Best of all is the first luscious pink rhubarb, crisp, and fatly bursting out of its Victorian pottery forcer.

It is also time for those eccentrics the Crown Imperials to flower. Eye-catching, and faintly ridiculous, the heavy heads of gold, or orange, bells are crowned by a tuft of strappy leaves, and the long purplish stems, with a bloom like damsons, twist about with no regard to the position of the sun, so that one wonders if they are gossiping together about the gardener behind her back. Beauty, however, is in the eye of the beholder: when these plants were first introduced to western Europe in the 1600s, from their home on the slopes of north India and Iran, the Persian name for them was Tears of Mary, a reference to the drop of nectar at the base of each petal. Christian tradition tells us that only the proud Crown Imperial failed to bow its head at the Crucifixion, but has, ever since, hung its head and wept in contrition.

Francis Bacon begins his essay on gardens: 'God Almighty

first planted a garden: and indeed it is the purest of human plea-
sures.' Later in the essay Bacon suggests that ideally one should
have a separate garden for each month of the year, which is indeed
a counsel of perfection, and he continues with a list of appropriate
plants for each month. Among his April suggestions are double
white violets, double peonies and 'lilies of all natures'. It must have
been warmer in the 1600s: there are no sign of lilies of any nature
in April, but how lovely it would be to grow double white violets.

Winter to spring

At the start of this month, the winter returned, after a brief relapse
into something resembling spring, with snow flurries. The snow
did not settle but, with frosts most nights, we were given a timely
reminder not to go headlong into a gardening spree just because
the clocks had been advanced an hour. For the first time for many
years, we did not pick our own daffodils to decorate the church
for Easter.

A few years ago I made the mistake of planting a *Leylandii*
hedge to give us privacy from the next-door barn conversion. The
main attraction of this cross is that it grows very rapidly and will
form a close-knit screen if clipped regularly. It has not proved a
good choice for a small garden. I have now given it the first clip,
and will try to repeat the exercise every two months or so. A glut-
ton for punishment, I also brought from our last garden a two-
foot-high seedling of the common yew, *Taxus baccata*, which is
now about 12 feet high. I have clipped this into a cone, providing
a reasonably weatherproof shelter for small birds, as well as for
the perennial nasturtium, *Tropaeolium speciosum.*

Even when the weather conditions are adverse, plants somehow
know the right time to start growing again. I have become con-

vinced over the years that, although temperature is a significant factor in plant growth, the lengthening of daylight hours is just as important. Professional growers produce flowers and plants out of season using their knowledge of the effects of such variables as temperature, light duration and light intensity on plant growth.

I like to see flowering shrubs and climbers growing against walls, for, carefully chosen, they can complement the architecture. Some people are not happy to plant shrubs against walls, because they fear damage to the foundations by the plant roots; but shrubs can be kept under control by careful pruning, and they will help to keep the walls dry by absorbing excess moisture from the soil. Be careful with the pruning of shrubs like forsythia, which do not flower on new wood.

Visiting gardens

I enjoy wandering round other people's gardens, as well as public gardens, parks, and botanical gardens, not just to admire the plants, the planting arrangements or the well-manicured lawns, but to notice how other people do things – or sometimes how they don't do them. In particular, I love discovering plants new to me. As I made my way round the University Botanical Garden in Oxford, I came across the widow iris, *Hermodactylus tuberosus*, in full bloom. It is, in fact, a genus of the iris family with only one species. I am not sure of the taxonomic characteristics which distinguish it from the other members of the family, but it is one of the earliest-flowering irises, a tuberous plant producing yellow-green flowers whose petals have very distinctive black tips, and whose long thin grey-green leaves have a distinctive square cross-section. It is completely hardy and I think deserves to be more widely known and grown.

Visiting friends in Sussex we were surprised to find that the spring growth was not more than a week or ten days ahead of us here in Cumbria. I had not been to Sussex for a few years, and was glad to see the recovery from the gale damage of 1989 and 1990. Natural phenomena such as gales, sea erosion, earthquakes and volcanic eruptions are usually regarded as national disasters against which precautions should be taken, but nature is not so easily foiled: in the end it is both easier and cheaper to work with her. The loss of majestic trees is sad, but visiting Wakehurst Place for the first time I was impressed to see the way in which the authorities of 'Kew in the Country' have seized the opportunity to reorganize the gardens on a geographical rather than a taxonomic grouping. For example, the steep-sided valleys, probably not dissimilar on a small scale to the Himalayan valleys, have provided an excellent site for the rhododendrons and azaleas, some of the former already in bloom.

Another plant which attracted my attention was in the rock garden, although I am not sure whether it is technically an alpine. It is the small, hardy perennial, spring-flowering pea, *Lathyrus vernus* var. *albo-roseus*. The true species has a very much darker, almost purple, flower. It only grows about 9–12 inches high, and forms a neat little clump of typical pea flowers with fern-like leaves.

Some of the most attractive spring-flowering shrubs are the witch hazels, with their unusual flower form; but not so well known are their near relatives, the members of the genus *Corylopsis*. *C. pauciflora* is probably the species most commonly seen, but one which caught my eye in Oxford was *C. spicata* from Japan. It was a mature specimen which had grown to about 7ft and developed a spread of 10ft, so it is not a shrub for a small garden. But the abundant 2ft-long racemes of pale yellow flowers were truly eye-catching.

47

Last May I was surprised and delighted to find my Chilean fire-tree, *Embethrium coccineum lanceslatum*, bearing a few brilliant scarlet flowers for the first time in the seven years since planting. Although it is said to be suitable only for the west and south-west of England, a far greater number of flower-buds are developing this year. We look forward to a striking splash of scarlet towards the end of May.

The flower garden

As I walk round the garden I notice that all sorts of plants have seeded in addition to the ubiquitous groundsel: aquilegia, *Viola cornuta* in varieties, *V. labradorica* and pansies in profusion. They will be potted up for sale, together with rooted offshoots of heuchera, hardy geraniums, Michaelmas daisies, phlox and lily of the valley.

What a pretty sight *Daphne mezereum* is with its cerise fragrant flowers close to the bare stems, but I think I am going to look out for *D. bhuola*, which flowers earlier and has large creamy inflorescense tinged pink. It is very strongly scented too.

I think my greatest thrill on our home return was to find that *Primula heucherifolia* was alive and well. This Asiatic primula is from Szechuan Province in western China, where it was collected by the famous Abbé David in 1869. It is not often seen in cultivation. It is distinguished by its leaves, which are roughly triangular and irregularly toothed like the garden heuchera – hence the name. It has a tall, slender stem carrying a single head of anything up to ten nodding mauve-pink-to-rich-purple flowers.

The kitchen garden

I am glad to see signs of green in the buds of the cuttings of gooseberries and red- and whitecurrants taken last autumn: they seem to be starting to root. The large clump of rhubarb doesn't look at all happy; it is about 15 years old and has probably outgrown its strength. The variety, Stockbridge Arrow, produces long, tender stems which are a rich red colour when young. When cooked it has a medium-sharp taste, without the acidity often associated with common rhubarb. But it has shown a marked tendency over the last two or three years to produce numerous flowerheads, which may have weakened it. The crowns of the variety Early Timperley planted two years ago are now well settled in, so even if Stockbridge Arrow does start to grow I'll probably take it out: the clump does take up rather too much space in a relatively small garden.

Two years ago I tried unsuccessfully to buy a fan-trained Victoria plum to plant against the south-facing wall of my neighbour's garage. All the nurserymen and garden centres told me that there was no call for such things. They didn't seem to appreciate my telling them that since I had asked for one there was a call. In the end I bought a young bush tree which is now being trained into a fan by judicious pruning and tying in – and incidentally saving me quite a bit of money.

In the herb garden the French parsley is throwing out lots of new leaves, but because I allowed it to seed itself last autumn there are hundreds of seedlings coming up all over the place. We prefer the French parsley mainly because of its milder flavour, but also because of its reliable growth: ordinary curled parsley can be very temperamental.

The vegetable garden looks rather forlorn just now. There is much to be done before sowing starts towards Easter. The sprouts are finished, and all the green growth will be stripped off and the stems sliced with a sharp knife as low as possible ready for the compost heap. I find that the inside of brassica stems are too soft to be dealt with by the shredder: it simply gets clogged. The roots will be burnt to avoid any transmission of clubroot. I am reminded also that two blackcurrant bushes must be taken out and burnt since they have big-bud – the extra large buds caused by the activities of a mite called *Cecidophyopsis ribis*. I have tried for two or three years to control it, but still it is there in the bushes, so reluctantly I must get rid of them.

We all tend to forget the names of plants. To help my recall I have started an indexed pocketbook in which I am listing plant names, where seen, and anything of special note.

The greenhouse and cold frame

The greenhouse is coming into its own now. The geraniums and fuchsias have all survived the winter, and with gentle watering are beginning to start into growth, so that in a few weeks' time more cuttings will be taken. Half-hardy cuttings taken last autumn of yellow and white argyranthemums, the mauve wallflower Erysimum Bowles Mauve, and several varieties of lavender and salvia, are well rooted and have recently been potted up individually. My stock plants of the dainty pale-blue *salvia patens* and the striking chocolate-coloured *Cosmos atrosanguinea*, which I feared lost, are beginning to throw up new shoots; so more cuttings to take later on.

Some of the herbaceous perennials need dividing, and this is a good time to do it. Any space pieces I have will be potted up for my annual charity plant sale in May. I also have self-sown seedlings of such plants as aquilegia, which are surplus to requirements, and I will pot these up as well.

The sowing of the bedding-plants is underway in the greenhouse. I find the differing requirements of varying species quite fascinating. Some, like the impatiens (Busy Lizzie), require a moist atmosphere in full light, so they are simply pressed into a pan of damp compost and placed in a polythene bag. Others, like those of antirrhinum, verbena and nemesia, prefer to be covered with a little compost of fine sand and kept in the dark until germination. In general, the larger the seed, the deeper the covering.

If it continues, the cold weather will soon cause a space problem in the greenhouse. Ideally I would like to put the half-hardy plants which have overwintered there into a cold frame to be covered with sacking at night to prevent frost damage. This would then make room for pricking out the annuals, which are germinating and need the warmth. But I am reluctant to make this move for a week or two yet.

I enjoy experimenting, and this year, in the hope of getting some really early peas, I sowed a dozen seeds of Feltham First in individual peat pots in gentle warmth. These are now about 4 inches high and have been hardened off in the cold frame, so they can be planted out shortly and covered with a fleece.

General tasks / Planning ahead

We had broken our journey south with a visit to Wisley. Seeing stone-flagged paths being relaid, and redevelopment going on in the boggy area below the reconstructed rock garden, I was reminded once again that from time to time our own gardens need examination and perhaps redesigning and replanting. Indoors we cheerfully redesign the kitchen, and have new carpets or curtains, but we consider the garden design to be permanent. It is good planning to look carefully at what we've got.

April

Flower for the month: Anemone

One day when the beautiful Adonis was hunting, he was savaged by a wild boar. As he lay dying, Venus, the goddess of all beauty, wept over him, and where her tears fell delicate white flowers sprang up: wild anemones, our wind-flowers; while from the blood flowing from Adonis's wounds grew crimson anemones, still used in the Gardens of Adonis created annually in Greece to celebrate the rebirth of the natural world, when Adonis returned from six months in the underworld, and all nature mourned.

Flowers for the house

Arranging flowers needs care in assessing the size of the room and the scope of the arrangement. It is easy to overpower a small room. April is a happy month for quick and easy small arrangements, and it is worth visiting a jumble sale or bric-à-brac stall to enlarge your supply of containers. It is also useful to use tiny jam jars or plain plastic containers to place inside a valuable vessel, and so avoid damage to a cut-glass dish or silver sugar bowl, for instance.

Wallflowers combine well with pottery and hardly need any arrangement; vivid forget-me-nots become special in glass; lilies of the valley stand well among their own leaves; huge pansy heads can be floated among leaves in a plain saucer.

If you wish to bring taller flowers into a small room, avoid crowding the vase and especially avoid too much foliage.

Flowers for the church

Flowers for church should be easy in the weeks after Easter: white lilies stay fresh for some time and will comfortably match up with whatever is available. It is a relief that there are no colour restrictions until Whitsun, except for the only too possible hazards of weddings. Anyone striving for consensus between the requirements of an increasingly captious bride, or brides, and the Vicar's standards of permitted church decoration needs to practise skills worthy of the diplomatic corps. Since wedding decor tends to follow waves of fashion, two brides may agree on a mutually acceptable colour scheme: it is less likely that they will understand that neither the font nor the pulpit is purpose-built as a container for giant flower arrangements. Hopefully it can be explained that lilies look wonderful for weddings, exhibit solid amounts of colour on long stems, last well, and are good value for money. Never be persuaded into decorating a whole church with freesias, or roses – the stuff of nightmares.

The children's garden – *Pools*

Even a tiny area of water adds to the attractions of a garden, particularly for birds who enjoy bathing. You will need to carry water, so site it reasonably near a tap.

If it is not too expensive, you can buy a fibre-glass container ready to be set in a carefully prepared depression. Mask the edge with a few stones and surround it with rockery plants. Pools need one or two aerating plants in them, to keep the water clean.

Alternatively, set an old-fashioned dustbin lid upside down in the ground, hold it steady with packed compost and stones, and plant it up. Thirdly, you could line a depression with butyl, again holding it in place with stones.

If you are lucky you might be creating a nursery for frogs.

Your library is sure to have a book which will give you ideas.

Tailpiece

It is a sheer delight to watch the antics of the coal tits, blue tits, chaffinches and robins as they feed on the nuts, coconut and crumbs put out on the bird-table, and to see them defending their position against starlings, rooks and the occasional crow; but it is quite a different matter to see the damage done to the flowering cherry *Prunus subhirtella*, and the gooseberries which are beginning to show bud, mostly by chaffinches; time to get the netting in place on the fruit cage.

Things to enjoy

- Alternating sun and showers, with cloud shadows sweeping over hills, moors and wolds.

- Hearing the first cuckoo.

- The first touches of colour on verges and motorway embankments.

- Spending some time in the garden over the Easter holiday.

- Looking out for magnolias and camellias, so often flourishing in square gardens, in tubs and in below-pavement areas in central London.

- The start of the gardens-open-to-the-public season. Plan to revisit old friends and explore some new ones.

May

Spring is sooner recognized by plants than men.

Whatever the weather, some arrivals never fail: the call of the first cuckoo; swifts moving at racing speed, flying straight as an arrow from south to north; and the flowering, in Scalby churchyard, of the rare *Cardamine bulbifera*, coralroot bitter-cress. Commonly called wormroot, this rather boring speciality can be relied on to flower in welcome to the bishop coming to confirm. One year the episcopal car collapsed on the wolds, which is not an area with a garage on every corner, so it was a small miracle that his lordship arrived, with complete composure, and fully robed, with five minutes to spare: but as a chorister drily suggested, the chances of hitching a lift must be well above average if you stand at the roadside in cope and mitre leaning on a crozier. Less welcome each year is the early appearance of that strapping country girl Blooming Sally – rosebay willow herb – sprawling across a path, where she is impervious to the strongest weedkiller. Gerard says this 'handsome plant deserves to be culti-vated': my herbal warns that 'an infusion of this plant produces stupefying results', which in Kamchatka are intensified in a popu-lar local brew that includes fly agaric. Travellers in far places should always be wary of what they drink.

May is a good time to celebrate with the last of the season's rum-pot and to begin a new brew with the first soft fruit. Rhubarb has rather too aggressive a flavour to blend well, but young gooseberries are acceptable, if they are sufficiently plentiful to spare from the freezer to ensure an all-year-round supply of that most delectable of English puddings, gooseberry fool.

The single-minded zealousness of the late convert applies to plants as well as to religion. I deplore the years wasted before I came to appreciate tulips. May is gourmet-feast time for tulip lovers: from window boxes to parks and gardens, so many different ways of planting all offer an exultant spectacle. Neat little Kaufmanniana appear quite humble as opposed to eye-catching parterres, planted, like immense patchwork quilts, with tens of thousands of bulbs, whose vibrant colours and stiff backs make an impressively haughty statement. Orange-flowered berberis makes an excellent background for the glowing colours of the Dutch Royal Family – Queen Wilhelmina, Queen Juliana, William of Orange, Dutch Princess, and Princess Irene – all in fiery combinations of gold, orange and salmon. For perfection include the complementing mahogany of Abu Hassan.

An ancient document says of the tulip: 'she is clean and well proportioned; her shape is like an almond; her inner petals are like a well … she is the chosen of the chosen' – and this is not a quotation from the Song of Songs.

A privileged way to enjoy nature in the surrounding countryside is high up in the passenger seat of a twenty-ton truck, and May is one of the best months to go 'cabbing' over the wolds, south of Scarborough when great sweeps of rolling country are glowing with the violent yellow of oil-seed rape; the softer gold of gorse on uncultivated banks and pale cowslips on the verges, where cow parsley is just frothing into flower. Rape is spoken of as a comparatively new crop, but I have seen an 1800 print illustrating how it was harvested, using a flail.

It is a common saying that 'kissing's out of fashion when the gorse is out of bloom', and indeed it is rarely that one cannot find a few cheerful gorse blooms. Whatever the distribution of gorse in the rest of Europe, it is recorded that when Linnaeus visited Britain and saw, for the first time, the full flowering in early summer, he wept for the beauty of it.

The flower garden

By now drier conditions have given me the opportunity to carry out a major overhaul of the main borders, the first for several years. A number of self-sown, bicoloured brooms, *Cytisus scoparius*, which had become too large to move to another spot or to pot up for sale, were dug out; and the overgrown *Philadelphus coronarius*, which should have been pruned last autumn, was thinned out, with care taken not to remove too much of the new growth, upon which flowering will occur in June and July. It is a useful shrub for a dry spot, and is more delicate and dainty than the more exuberant hybrids commonly associated with the name Mock Orange. The shrubby *Potentilla fruticosas* were tackled next, as they had spread too far over paths and garden. Until recently the commonest forms of this useful shrub were in shades of white and of yellow, since the development of orange and red forms had eluded the plant breeders; but success came about two or three decades ago with the introduction of Red Ace, the first truly red *P. fruticosa*. I have both Red Ace and Tangerine. It is important to prune old wood and weak stems right back to ground level to encourage new growth. Stems which are simply short-ened tend to die off.

The next victim of the secateurs was the rambler rose, which has been with us since we lived in Sheffield 30 years ago. Its name is not known to me, but it usually covers a trellis bordering our boundary front wall with a mass of pale-cream double flowers in July. It hasn't been pruned for about three years, the main reason for my neglect being that there are two clematis plants on the same trellis; they make a very effective display with the rose. It proved quite easy to disentangle them. The clematis are *C. Marie Boisselot*, with its beautiful large white flowers, and *C. viticella Minuet*, whose flowers are dainty white and mauve and look like the bells of campanulas. The scarlet-flowered honeysuckle, *Lonicera brownii*, is there as well to provide an additional splash of strong and distinctive colour.

My main task has been to move a small *Acer palmatum* tree bought as a seedling for 25p some years ago at a charity garden sale. It has since grown to about 4ft 6in. high, with a similar spread, and was too big for its position. It was possible to lever it out on to a plastic sheet and drag it to its new position. When it was securely in place I sank two 6-inch diameter earthenware drainpipes into the ground on either side. These will be filled with water twice daily for the next six months to allow the tree to recover fully from its move and get its roots re-established.

The early dwarf rhododendrons are coming into bloom, and being mainly bright red provide a vivid contrast with the late daffodils. When planting rhododendrons I first dig out a hole, the diameter of which is at least four times that of the container in which the plant came. It is then filled with a lime-free compost, consisting of 40-per-cent composted bark, 40-per-cent sterilized loam, and ten-per-cent silver sand. This gives a good open mixture with a pH acceptable to the plants, and very similar to that of their natural environment in the Himalayas. They also need some shelter from windy conditions, at least until they are fully established.

We are very fond of forsythia, and its mass of yellow flowers in early spring is a most welcome sight among the flowering shrubs. Recently I read that it is possible to grow forsythia as a standard shrub on a single stem, so as soon as my specimen has finished flowering I will select a strong straight stem, tie it to a stake and remove the other stems at ground level. With careful pruning I hope to be able to finish up with a shapely head which can be controlled in future years with an annual haircut after flowering.

The borders are beginning to show more colour with *Dicentra spectabilis* (bleeding heart), both pink and white; the yellow *Doronicum cordatum* and its double form, Spring Beauty; and the polyanthus hybrids. They all add their colour to that of the daffodils. I have a clump of the lovely *Ipheion uniflorum*, which is a member of the lily family, giving a mass of blue colour. It will continue to bloom here throughout the next few months. I find it perfectly hardy, and it thrives well in the partial shade of a small rose bed.

Unfortunately the cold winds from the north, together with the frequent frosts of the last few weeks, have damaged the early growth on the *Dicentra*, and the tender new shoots of the *Acer palmatum dissectum atropurpureum* are looking very sad. Two years ago I planted *Osmanthus delavayi*, a compact evergreen shrub with dark green ovate leaves. It is blooming for the first time. The mass of white tubular flowers is very fragrant, but it has needed night-time protection: the old lace curtains have come in very useful.

The lawn is beginning to recover from my efforts to eradicate moss. Unfortunately my solution of Jeyes Fluid was too concentrated: while it effectively killed the moss it also severely scorched the newly growing grass. After I had removed the dead moss with a hired electric lawn rake the lawn looked a very sorry sight. So beware: Jeyes is excellent, but, as with all chemicals, the instructions must be closely followed.

Once more the importance of position to give the best results has been demonstrated: the hyacinths and tulips in the window boxes at the back of the house were not only earlier than those at the front, but are of better quality, although all received the same treatment and were put in position at the same time. Those at the back face south-west, whilst those at the front of the house face north-east and get only the early-morning sun.

A wet winter will take its toll of the species primulas. Although they are moisture-lovers, they do not like our winter wet, and really should be given the protection of a glass-plate cover from autumn to spring. In their native habitat, either in alpine Europe or in the mountains of Asia, they are covered through the winter months with deep snow, which provides considerable protection from alternating hard frosts and wet around their crowns.

Great strides have been made in recent years in developing new strains of polyanthus, two of which – Pacific Giant hybrids from the USA, and the Regal strain from Tasmania – are superb. The polyanthus must be amongst the earliest cultivated herbaceous hybrid plants, originating as a natural cross between the cowslip (*primula veris*) and the primrose (*primula acaulis*), thus producing the common oxlip, the first coloured forms of which were described in 1665, and from which was developed the polyanthus we know today.

There is a form of one-up-manship which occurs in almost all keen gardeners, namely the knowledge that they have a plant which most of their neighbours do not, and I am no exception to this. A few weeks ago a new gardening friend brought me a plant which was completely new to me; I was even unable to track it down in my reference books. It is obviously a member of the borage family, and looks like a dwarf pulmonaria, with similar, very rough, lanceolate leaves, and has inflorescences like pulmonaria, except that they are yellow. It was labelled *Nonea setosa roem* and had apparently come in an exchange of seedlings from a botanical garden in eastern France. I am planting it in a damp, shaded part of the garden and will watch its development with interest and care, but in the meantime I have a distinct feeling of superiority.

The new plants I ordered a couple of months ago have arrived, and homes are ready for them. I do admire the skill with which nurserymen pack plants for carriage these days. They had all obviously been well watered before packing in plastic bags with string tops, which were then surrounded with masses of shredded paper for protection in a very stout cardboard box.

I ordered two shrubs. One was the spring-flowering *Exocorda macrantha*, the Bride, which bears prolific pure-white flowers in racemes against leaves of a light to medium green. It grows 5–6 feet all round, and can easily be kept in check by judicious pruning after flowering. The other was a very small cherry, *Prunus incisa Kojo-no-mai*, which I understand is the Japanese for 'dance of the butterflies'. It is described as providing year-round interest, so it will be planted in a container on the rear patio; but it will probably be necessary to give the container at least some protection from winter weather.

The other plants are for the herbaceous border, and extend the range of the pentstemons. I've added the crimson-scarlet King George and the white Snowstorm; and to the *Phlox paniculata* I've added Blue Ice, whose pink buds open to white flowers tinged with blue; Prospero, with large pale purple flowerheads; and Starfire, a beautiful deep red. Then for the front of the border a clump of the viola Mollie Sanderson, whose distinctive midnight blue-black flowers are characterized by a small golden-yellow eye, and another clump of the viola Jackanapes, with yellow and maroon flowers. As the summer proceeds, cuttings will be taken of these new plants to overwinter in the frames as an insurance for a stock next year.

Last year I acquired two specimens of the small shrub False Heather (*Cuphea hyssopifolia*) which, as may be supposed, has leaves which can quite easily be mistaken for hyssop. It has prolific small tubular flowers which can range from white through pink to dark red, and I have one white and one red. Like the more common *C. ignea* (sometimes called the Cigar Plant from its yellow-tipped red flowers), *C. hyssopifolia* is only half-hardy, and is best grown in the greenhouse. Mine are now bursting into growth, and the big surprise is the volume of seed which they have produced.

The kitchen garden

In the kitchen garden a fan-trained greengage has been planted on the south-facing wall alongside the Victoria plum. Greengages can be shy to pollinate, and the Victoria plum is generally regarded as best for this purpose.

The broad beans and the first peas are now sown and protected by polythene-sheet cloches, which will also help to warm up the soil. I have also sown parsnips, and then beetroot, turnips and Swiss chard. This last does better with us than spinach and has the advantage of the celery-like stems – excellent for soups.

I have been very busy recently because last autumn I decided to dig up my raspberries which, although only three years old, were not thriving. Because of shortage of space in the fruit cage, I decided to plant the new canes in the same place as the old – with two differences. First, I changed the soil; and second, as an experiment, I decided to improve the drainage by growing them on a raised bed. I collected first-class certified canes from a Scottish grower just before Christmas, but because of the weather they have remained heeled in the ground until last week. I prepared the ground well by digging a deep trench, incorporating a thick layer of well rotted manure and another of good friable compost, and capping all with new soil. The raised part is contained with concrete building-blocks set on edge, so that the soil level of the raspberry planting is about 9 inches above garden level. This will provide a well drained growing site, but since raspberries need plenty of moisture I will need to make sure they do not dry out. The canes have been planted some months too late, but I hope that they will quickly settle and produce good fruiting-canes for next year.

The greenhouse and cold frame

I've had a slight mishap with the seed potatoes. They were sprouting nicely up until Easter on the spare bedroom bed. We then had visitors for about ten days, so the potatoes had to be moved into the smallest bedroom, which has less daylight. The result is potatoes with shoots up to 6 inches in length, which will have to be planted very carefully to avoid breakage. I'm growing Arran Pilot and Sharpe's Express again this year, as our soil seems to suit them well. I've given up maincrop potatoes, mainly because I haven't the space to grow them.

Pricking out the bedding plants – asters, antirrhinums, stocks, nemesia, etc. – is now in full swing. As soon as they have recovered from the shock of transplanting and begun to make good growth they will be moved out into the new cold frames, which are already easing the congestion in the greenhouse. The plants will then be hardened off and be ready, I hope, for my annual plant sale. Although the warm weather of a few weeks ago brought everything on more quickly, I am hesitant to put much out to harden off yet.

A recent task has been to oversee the erection by our local builder of the new lean-to greenhouse at the back of the house. Quite a lot of garden reorganization was required – like lifting and transplanting a hybrid rhododendron, Peeping Tom; moving the purple-flowered and berried *Callicarpa bodinieri* var. *giraldii*; and transferring two clumps of *Lilium candidum* into large clay pots to stand on the patio. The greenhouse will be heated, and we are planting a peach on the wall which faces south-south-west; perhaps a grape vine as well. The staging will be used mainly for bringing on flowering plants. This will release the greenhouse in the kitchen garden solely for germination of seeds in spring, and tomatoes, cucumbers and peppers in the summer.

Outside, the sweet-peas which were sown in February are now hardening off in the cold frame. In addition to the usual Spencer types, and the very old variety called Matucana, I'm also trying the dwarf variety Pink Cupid in some of the window boxes.

General tasks

The birds have had a wonderful time during the last few weeks foraging round the garden for suitable material for their nests. Most notable were the antics of the jackdaws, attacking the loose ends of the twine tying the climbing and rambler roses on the pergola: presumably the soft fibre makes a suitable lining material for the nests. It has been a relatively mild winter: the blackbirds and thrushes seem to be actively ferreting out slugs and snails, while the tits like to search out small insects and the aphids which I see are appearing already on the roses. I am happy for them to continue, but trust that the finches will not make too much mess of the blossoms.

After pruning the shrubs all the waste material has been shredded to make a welcome addition to the compost heap. I really wonder how I managed before I was given my shredder by a group of friends just over two years ago. I have once more spread composted bark to a depth of about 3–5 inches over about a third of the borders to help improve the soil texture. This also has the effect of an added bonus by providing a mulch to aid the control of annual weeds; but it does nothing to deter the perennial pests like dandelion, ground elder and creeping thistle. If these can't be dug out, then continued, patient and repeated application of a herbicide may be necessary; but care must be taken not to touch the leaves of the border plants, and of course to follow the manufacturer's instructions implicitly.

Flower for the month: *Myosotis* – Forget-me-not

In May one thinks of Chaucer, Shakespeare and a nostalgic era of chivalry, colour and romance far different from the pain, dirt and smells of reality. Surprisingly, neither Shakespeare nor Chaucer mention forget-me-nots which seem to blend perfectly with 'daisies pied and violets blue'. Less surprisingly, their shapely sprays of tiny blue flowers are not beloved of poets, perhaps because of their cumbersome name, though Coleridge bravely writes of 'Hope's gentle gem, the sweet forget-me-not'.

It is told that a German knight walking beside a river with his lady reached towards some beautiful blue flowers and fell into the rushing water. His elaborate court clothes pulled him down, but as he was drowning he managed to throw the flowers at his lady's feet, crying, *'Vergiss mein nicht!'* – Forget me not, or as Redouté names his famous painting, *Le ne m'oubliez pas*. Long names for small flowers.

Flowers for the house

May is the month to wallow in tulips: long before the Dutch organized a futures market to trade in their precious bulbs, the Turkish gift of love was a red tulip, our lily-flowered variety with elegant dagger-shaped petals.

Of all flowers tulips will arrange themselves; prepare an accurate design of stiff buds and in a few hours you will have a charming pattern of open faces twisting and curving in great beauty.

May is the month to have fun copying Dutch flower paintings. Tulips, with peonies; hyacinths; columbines; narcissi; bunnera; Crown Imperials, and fritillaries – all look wonderful massed in a brass pot, but you will never pack in as many blooms as those old masters painted.

Flowers for the church

If you rely on garden flowers for church decoration May is a promising month. Lilac should be prolific – white shows up better than purple, and will need some of its foliage stripping. Dutch iris are amenable, but again, beware of blues and purples which tend to 'vanish' in church. Yellow or white iris look particularly striking among the range of flame, orange and gold broom; though if the church is small the smell can be overpowering. New foliage on trees and shrubs is at its best, but will droop if not put quickly into water.

May also covers some major festivals: the feast of the Transfiguration, usually white; Trinity, without colour restrictions; and Whitsun, white and red. No problem with white – spinaea arguta, white tulips, deutzia, viburnum and osmanthus are available; but will red peonies be ready?

The children's garden – *An arbour*

Long ago our ancestors enjoyed sitting, and playing games, in the sun. Their choice of seats was limited but they created arbours, sheltered corners protecting a grass-covered mound to sit on. This could still be made, especially if you are permitted to use a section of fence, or hedge, as a backing up which to grow climbing plants; roses, clematis, sweet peas, nasturtiums are all suitable. The grass-covered bank is not easy, but you could use a hefty log as a seat, or planks resting on bricks at each end; or even an old chair or stool might be spared.

For privacy you should grow some plants at each side to form a wing. This could be shorter everlasting sweet peas, supported by sticks; or a plastic container, planted with tall perennials; or if tall canes are available, train some climbing plants up them and across the top to form a roof. Anything growing near a hedge dries out quickly, so remember to water often.

Things to enjoy

- The burst of colour in urban districts. Parks and gardens departments excel themselves in May, with beds of tulips and wallflowers and all the pinks and whites of hawthorn, cherry and crab in extravagant bloom.

- The peak of the dawn chorus – do song birds ever go to bed?

- Mixing up packets of annual seeds in your hand and scattering them where they are to flower, on a warm wet day.

- Drifts of bluebells flowering under the bright soft green of new leaves in a beech wood.

- Taking time, in a busy month, to look at your own garden, and talk about gardens with your friends.

June

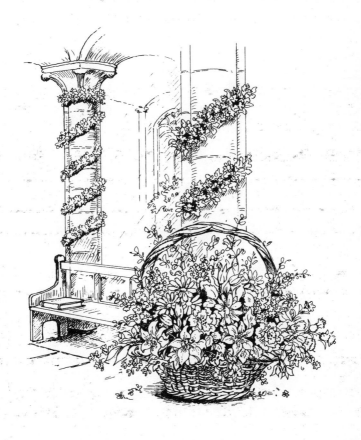

What we loved best about England was the grass – the short, clean, incredibly green grass with its underlying tough springy turf, three hundred years growing.

(Han Suyin)

A mild annoyance for vicarage gardeners, once the weather is warm enough for wedding parties to dawdle in the churchyard with their photographers, are the winds which blow the confetti into our gardens. The wretched stuff is mostly indestructible, cannot be swept from gravel, or collected from flower beds, and makes an unsightly mess.

How different is the sensational carpet of pink and white blossom which the same breezes blow off the fruit trees. Now, as the new fruit sets, is the time to prepare one of the most truly romantic gifts. We all know about Eve's disastrous offering to Adam; but what about the chivalrous knight who presents his lady with an apple enclosing a pearl, jewel or coin? Simply press your chosen favour into the bud end of the fruit and leave the gift wrapping to nature. You must remember which apple is so loaded, and also hope that your orchard is not ravaged by the attentions of an escaped parakeet, as happened some years ago in Scalby.

As the yellows of spring fade we drift into the blue/pink/purple phase of midsummer: gentle blue periwinkles crawl under the trees; spreading ceanothus complement the starry spikes of camassia; deep blue perennial cornflowers lie about in the hedge-bottoms; and royal blue monkshood contrasts with the soft grey-blue of rosemary. Sir Thomas Moore wrote: 'As for Rosemarine I lette it runne all over my gardens walls, not only because my bees love it, but it is the herb sacred to remembrance.'

One gold which is welcome to intrude into the summer blues is the very early flowering Rosa Primula, the incense rose. The small, cup-like flowers are the gentlest shade of gold; the thorns are menacing, but the perfume, on a hot day, is redolent of high anglican ritual: candles, bells, thuribles, and cassocks full of buttons.

Scalby, like many other parishes, has, for a number of years, celebrated midsummer with a Fair and Flower Festival. By early June the scene is already set, with immaculate gardens, and baskets and tubs flowering in every available space along the High Street. Teams of volunteers help out the sextons so that the churchyard will look its best. Someone will have to think up a theme for the flower festival which the vicar, who rightly insists on a Christian message, will accept. This leaves the vicar's wife to pray for just sufficient rain (watering takes up valuable time), no wind, no temperament from the lawnmower, a fine day, no accidents with the boiling urns in the garden, no disasters with her scones, peace among the flower arrangers, and inspiration to interpret some impossible theme with flowers, a lasting mortification being the memory of the year of Gregorian chant – too many neumes and too many flowers.

Like hens laying astray, some plants seem to manage better on their own. Every year the most striking aquilegias, dancing fairies, flower in a horrid tangle of goosegrass and nettles; the prettiest pink peony will only perform in a jumble of Solomon's Seal, false frankincense; and together these quite hide the lilies of the valley. Nearby blue and white campanulas compete with the sweet rocket. People say that sweet rocket should be weeded out – maybe, but at dusk on a warm June evening it gives out the most ravishing perfume in the garden. If these two plants had voices they would sing together 'anything you can do, I can do better'.

Amid so much horrific and contentious news an oddment of lighter reportage is welcome. The story of the great Burnley topers arises from the First World War, when the East Lancashire Regiment was stationed near Fécamp, and quickly discovered the sustaining power of Benedictine, that inspired brew of honey, herbs and spices, produced from a secret recipe of Dom Bernardo Vincelli, since 1510. A Second World War posting of the East Lancashires reinforced the habit so firmly in the next generation, that now the Burnley Working Men's Club is the monastery's largest retail outlet in the world. A former builder claims that after fifty years imbibing, a bottle a day helps him to sleep, and settles his stomach: and who is to say that the men of Burnley are not demonstrating a due appreciation of God's bounty from the apiary and herb garden?

'Dry sunny conditions'

Most of April and early May was wet, cold and thoroughly miserable, but the weather forecasters suddenly announced that on Thursday they could promise dry, sunny conditions with temperatures up to the low twenties centigrade. The age of miracles is not past: for once they were right, and the transformation in the gardens has indeed been miraculous over the past fortnight, as it is only now that the ground has dried out enough to give a good tilth for sowing the smaller seeds like carrots, turnips and beetroot, and been warm enough to produce a fairly quick germination. The onion sets I planted only a week ago are already two inches high.

It was comforting to find a retired professional gardener not far away confirming that the soil has not been fit to plant, and that only now was he contemplating planting up his kitchen garden. I feel I am in good company.

The flower garden

I am not in a hurry to put out the bedding plants, or indeed any of the cabbage family in the kitchen garden. They will come to no harm in their boxes for a week or two yet, and in any case the wallflowers are just at their best.

Our village is fairly exposed, at about 700 feet above sea level, on a thinnish covering of glacial deposits overlying hard carboniferous limestone. This gives a great variation in soil type even within the village. Only a few miles away is a warmer sandstone soil above the red Penrith sandstone. The contrast in plant development is most noticeable. I think the contrasts resulting from variations in height above sea level, aspect and the nature of the underlying geology over comparatively short distances are more noticeable in these northern areas.

The *Wisteria sinensis* is a mass of racemes in bud, and will come into flower in about a fortnight. Wisteria can be reluctant to bloom, and I have found pruning the new shoots back to two buds will encourage blossom formation.

All gardeners like to have at least one plant which is slightly exotic and which their neighbours do not possess. In my case blooming just now is *Arisaema consanguineum* – a small, bulbous arum-like plant with a brownish-red spath protecting the white spadix, which thrives in a humus-rich soil in partial shade. It looks exotic, even weird, and is a good talking-point with visitors.

I find that it pays to talk to plants. About five years ago I planted *Lonicera tatarica*, a shrubby member of the honeysuckle family from southern Russia and Turkestan; and it has been most reluctant to flower. Last autumn I told it that if it didn't do better it would have to go. The bush, about five feet high and three across, is now a mass of bright red inch-long flowers which show off well against the dark green foliage.

I often wonder whether to mark the position of plants which die down completely during the winter months. In the early spring I am liable to dig up plants when preparing a 'suitable site' for a new acquisition. This year it was *Fritillaria meleagris* which was attacked, and yet it went on to give the best display for years. Then again, we wondered whether *Incarvillia delavayii* had survived, for it didn't seem to be where we thought it had been last year; but we found that the nearby rosemary had become significantly larger and *I. delavayii* has appeared during the last week, growing as strongly as ever but partially under the rosemary. Overall I think markers will go in this year.

The Himalayan blue poppies must be a magnificent sight blooming in their native habitat, for there is no other plant whose blue stands out so vividly, not even among the delphiniums. These popular *Meconopsis* were introduced into British gardens only 70 years ago, and some of the finest varieties are found in the moist conditions of north-west England and Scotland. They are reputedly lime-haters, but mine are now established and appear to tolerate the amount of lime in our soil, though they do enjoy an annual mulch of composted bark or peat. Just now we are waiting for *Meconopsis regia* to come into bloom. As the name suggests, it is tall (about 5–6 feet) and stately, with large, soft, downy leaves, and a mass of yellow blooms. At the other end of the scale is the dainty harebell poppy, *M. quintuplinerva*, whose lavender-blue bells tinged with purple nod gracefully in the breeze.

Years ago I used to grow a lot of long-spurred hybrid aquilegias which, when mass-planted, gave a wonderful kaleidoscope of soft blue, pink, yellow and cream. They are, however, very susceptible to greenfly, and as such are not very desirable as cut flowers for the house. More recently, I have picked out a few of the species varieties, and one or two species crosses, to grow as specimen plants. One of the most beautiful of these is the *A. alpina/A. vulgaris* cross, Hensol Harebell, which is presently in bloom and attracting attention with its deep-Wedgwood-blue petals. My specimen appears the more striking because it grows next to the pure white, robust *Primula chionantha*. It is one of the more drought-resistant species, and deserves to be more widely grown.

Gardeners, like proud parents, repeatedly talk of their wonderful offspring, and so once again I must tell of my Chilean firetree, *Embothrium coccineum*, which is now in full flower. It stands about eight feet high, and is a mass of brilliant scarlet flowers. It is a really eye-catching sight, in association with a single white lilac which grows on one side of it, and *Stranvaesia davidiana*, whose leaves are variegated in white, pale orange, and green, on the other.

There have been several pleasant discoveries in the garden this year. Two or three years ago *Lychnis flos-jovis* disappeared, as did *Salvia turkestanica*. But recently I discovered with delight that seedlings have appeared around the positions of the original plants which look as if they are offspring. Another surprise was to discover several seedlings around an orange hybrid *Potentilla fruticosa*. They will be moved to a nursery bed and watched with interest.

One of the rewards of not being too tidy in the garden is the appearance of wonderful collections of seedlings in the borders. They include in my garden *Daphne mezereum*, *Actea rubra*,

Heuchera Palace Purple (which I grow primarily for its heart-shaped deep purple leaves), and various varieties of broom and geranium. Last year's broom seedlings are now flowering for the first time, and among them are two that are a brilliant red and yellow, and one that is a deep red, almost maroon. Brooms are notorious for not breeding true from seed, and these certainly do not resemble our original plants. Tempting though it is to the tidy gardener to keep the hoe moving in the herbaceous and shrub borders, I'm not sure it is always a good idea. In the end, laborious hand weeding may be more profitable, for then one has a chance to distinguish weed seedlings from these free gems – not always an easy task.

Recently I have moved some plants which did not seem to be too happy in their positions, even though the garden is relatively small and one would think that one place was as good as another. *Callicarpa bodinieri giraldii* from China is one of these, for it is not entirely hardy and doubtless does better in the south of England. The main attraction of this small-to-medium-sized shrub is not the pale purple flowers, which are relatively insignificant, but the clusters of violet berries produced in the autumn. My specimen has now been moved into the rear garden and put against the south-facing wall, where it seems to be taking on a new lease of life, throwing out strong new growth and appearing much happier.

At the end of May, and indeed well into June, there is always the danger of ground frost at night, which can do untold damage to plants brought on in the greenhouse ready for planting: bedding plants, runner beans, marrows and courgettes are all susceptible. The main danger from frost is not so much the actual temperature, but the dew freezing on the leaves and then thawing fairly rapidly when the early sun melts the rime. Plants which have a thin layer of cellulose to their leaves, and those which are very fleshy like cacti and succulents, are the most susceptible. As a first line of defence I find that horticultural fleece does very well, and I have been covering my plants at night.

The warm spell just after Easter encouraged early growth, especially on oaks and acers, as well as the small trees and shrubs. I do think that cold winds and wind-frosts can do far more damage than just very low temperatures, for the winds tend to dehydrate the plants. Since the ground was already very dry at the time, they suffered from considerable water-loss just when they needed it most. The most dramatic damage I've seen to early foliage around here has been to the oaks at the National Trust property at Acorn Bank, Temple Sowerby, near Penrith, which is famed for its magnificent herb garden. A few miles away, at a large garden near Great Salkeld, a mature species acer, some 10m high, had all its new leaves blasted and shrivelled.

The kitchen garden

The new strawberry plants, Cambridge Favourite, are looking good and are full of blossom, having benefited from the generous layer of compost underlying them. The variety Tantallon will be taken up after fruiting, and I can only hope that this year they will produce runners: they failed to do so last year. I have just bought a few plants of the late variety Aromel. In order that they get properly established and make really good plants before fruiting, I have removed all the flower stalks.

The new raspberry canes have settled in, and are producing strong canes to fruit in the new year, but we will have to rely on pick-your-own fruit farms for raspberries and strawberries this summer.

I managed to get my Victoria plum and the greengage, growing as fan-trained trees against the northern boundary wall and fence of the kitchen garden, covered with fleece just as they came into flower. This stopped any damage from late frosts and there has been a good set of fruit. In fact, the Victoria plum is so heavy with swelling fruit that I will have to do some thinning to get good big plums, and to prevent the spurs carrying the fruit from breaking under the weight. The currants likewise were covered up and are developing a good crop. The main difficulty here was to secure the fleece sufficiently to stop it from being blown away.

The broad beans which I started in the greenhouse are coming into flower, and I will be sowing another row shortly outside to follow on. I will be planting out the runner beans too, also started indoors, in about ten days' time. The early potatoes are through, and this year I am experimenting with covering a few rows with black polythene to save the labour of earthing up and also of digging to harvest.

General tasks

One of the benefits of a hard winter as well as a late spring seems to be the control of insect pests. Normally by the end of May there are signs of attacks by the gooseberry sawfly caterpillars, which can completely defoliate a bush in a couple of days; but over the last few days I have kept a close watch on my gooseberries and on the red- and blackcurrants, and am pleased to find that their foliage looks clean and healthy, with no sign of aphids. Likewise, the roses are clear of greenfly so far.

However, whitefly has appeared again in the old greenhouse, so I am trying bright yellow sticky cards to combat them. Apparently whitefly are attracted to the colour yellow, so the cards are hung just above the affected plants. After one day, I am most impressed with the number of flies trapped on the glue. If this old method is successful, it will certainly be cheaper than some of the sprays on the market, which seem to me to encourage the breeding of resistant strains. Some of the less strong sprays merely give the whiteflies a refreshing bath.

Flower for the month: *Rosa* – Rose

Of all flowers the rose must appear most frequently in poetry, literature, art, embroidery, Christian symbolism and, of course, gardens in nearly every country in the world.

A basket of roses is the emblem of one little known martyr, St Dorothy, a Christian from Caesarea, who was arrested during Diodetian's persecution. In prison she converted all who were sent to pervert her, and she was sentenced to be beheaded. As she was led to her death, a lawyer, mocking her, asked her to send him heavenly fruit. Even as he spoke a child appeared carrying a basket of roses and apples, which Dorothy gave to the lawyer, who in his turn was converted, and eventually martyred.

Flowers for the house

There are probably more garden flowers to cut for the house in June than in any other month, which is just as well, since, unless one lives in a cool, stone-built house, they only last a few days. June is also the time for the first flush of roses and sweet peas: those loveliest, and most gracious of flowers, whose perfume breathes the very essence of English summer. Sweet peas need so little arranging: they are perfect loosely bunched and gently dropped into a narrow glass, with perhaps a little gypsophila to soften the edges. Whatever you do with roses they are gorgeous – in tight bud, full blown, floating heads, or in a bowl of mixed flowers where they will 'lift' the whole arrangement.

While the full range of herbaceous plants and summer bulbs are ready for large displays in June, keep them deadheaded, and the side shoots will be equally effective in small arrangements supporting pinks, mignonette and dainty rockery flowers.

Flowers for the church

With luck, weddings, and gardens, should provide all the flowers for the church in June, and since they are usually arranged on Friday or Saturday it is not important that all the tall herbaceous flowers, in light colours, will quickly drop and make work for the cleaners, who are sure to grumble. Lupins, larkspur, delphiniums, cornflowers, straight-stemmed alliums, star-like camassia and iris will all add grace and gentle colour to Sunday services. It is well worth growing giant spiraea and long-stemmed pale-yellow scabious, but be careful they do not take over your garden. A patch of onions left to flower is useful; home grown sweet williams have much longer stems than bought ones, but the dark shades can disappear in a dark church – fortunate the flower arrangers who work in the vast light churches of East Anglia. In the darker north great sprays of mock orange look wonderful. Many years ago I remember seeing Beverley Minster decorated entirely with huge pots of cow parsley. They probably made a sticky mess on the floor but against the austere stone the effect was magical.

Above all, beware the bride who wants roses all the way and 'knows someone who grows them'. Disaster. Florist's roses are difficult and garden roses impossible.

The children's garden – *Herb garden*

If you enjoy food and delicious smells, you should plan a herb garden: it is really exhilarating to pick your own herbs for cooking. You could make this in any shaped patch of earth, with a few stepping stones for convenience, or in a design of pots up the sides of steps. Herbs thrive in a sunny position, and if they are in pots will need watering regularly.

Some of the most useful plants to include are mint, any of several different flavours; parsley, to go with fish; chives, to liven cheese sandwiches; coriander, for soup; basil for tomato salad; with an edging of thyme all round.

Some of the larger plants are quite spectacular: cucumber-flavoured borage; liquorice-flavoured fennel; tarragon and lads' love. Include a bush of rosemary and one of sage if you have space, and if you can find one or two plants of salad bowl lettuce you can pick and eat the leaves all summer and they will continue to grow.

Tailpiece

I wonder if rabbits are becoming a nuisance in other parts of the country? I have a cheeky little fellow who calmly sits on the lawn and watches us have breakfast. My border terrier, Barney, seems to think this rabbit is hiding behind a stack of sacks of composted bark, and as a result is trying to tear them apart – and succeeding. I just hope that the rabbit will not migrate to the kitchen garden. I like to share produce with my neighbours, but there are limits.

Things to enjoy

- Light nights and the delectable perfume of sweet rocket at edge o'dark.

- Cow parsley frothing along the verges, and wild roses sprawling over hedges.

- The opportunity to visit gardens offering a charity garden trail.

- Looking out for plant stalls at village fairs, or open gardens.

- The first flowering of new roses, in your own garden, or at a show.

- The flowers, often pink and blue, of any church or cathedral celebrating its patronal festival at Petertide.

- Clouds of creamy elder flowers: cook several heads with young gooseberries for a muscatel flavour, and make refreshing elder flower champagne. Gooseberries and elder flowers are always ready together, however early or late the season.

July

Flowers leave some of their fragrance on the hand that bestows them.

July is the month for visitors, garden trails, roses, and, of course, the peculiar bliss of English gardens: the herbaceous border. As plants burgeon it becomes too crowded to weed, but cutting back lupins and delphiniums leaves room for side shoots to grow, and space for Canterbury bells, lilies and irises to elbow their way into the sun. Towards the front of the border the annual miracle takes place: a scatter of seeds on a warm, damp day produces a colourful tangle of pink and blue echiums, candytuft, Queen Anne's thimbles, miniature forget-me-not, hearts-ease, creeping campanula and love-in-a-mist.

Whatever the climatic vagaries, some plants, like true friends, are always generous performers, and most reliable of these is a lone delphinium plant, which somehow established itself, inconveniently near the path, in the lower garden. Each year it yields cuttings, has chunks of root sliced off, but notwithstanding it gets larger, and more floriferous each year. Recalling, with distaste, the tank of ox blood mixture brewed to feed delphiniums in my childhood home, I am reminded that my huge clump grows well below the level of the churchyard, and no doubt enjoys its family's macabre appetite. Another dependable stalwart is aquilegia, by whatever name it is known: eagles' claws, Grannie's bonnets, dancing fairies and other local variations. These old-fashioned favourites are great inter-breeders, so each year produces different colour combinations. One of the largest each year, as well as the prettiest, slurping nourishment, I suspect, from dubious kitchen plumbing, is in two shades of soft yellow, with white claws tipped by a yellow dot. Just as pretty are the self-seeds appearing all over the garden, reverting to their original, more compact shape, and to self-coloured pink or purple. The special gift of an old-style, starry-pink Norah Barlow plant, cosseted in a carefully chosen position, quickly disappeared. Provoking creature – next year she bloomed amid the strawber-ries, cuddling up to a pampas, and one immensely tall plant grew up the middle of a fuschia.

Apart from invited guests July always brings those one could do without. No doubt the Egyptians' plague of lice was worse than our annual infestation of woodlice: breeding under the carpet edges, under every stone in the garden, among the soft-fruit and in the larder. Jackdaws nesting on top of the chimneys throw pieces of sooty nest into the drawing room hearth, the creeper invades the roof space, and bats, whose radar is supposed to be so accurate, end up in the bedrooms. At least the Egyptians were spared megowlets, the original 'things that go bump in the night'. They are great brown beetles with sinister fringes, and their fear-some visitations usually take the form of crash-landing on the pillow, where they remain far-welted, or upside down as a stranded sheep does.

Garden trails are an enjoyable way both to raise money for charity and to spend an afternoon. Even if it rains the preparations are not wasted. Scalby is fortunate in having a natural progression through ten contrasting gardens, beginning and ending in the Church Rooms, where parking space and refreshments are avail-able. Number one is our own beautifully cared for churchyard, with its mature trees, five hundred or more graves, conservation area and vicar's goats. Through the vicarage garden to number three, where a courtyard, perfumed with apricot and gold azaleas, shelters a cake stall, and the 'quarter deck' gives a good view of banks of rhododendrons.

From there the trail continues to a most secluded garden: stone paths winding between giant copper beeches, with plenty of shade plants offset by bright colour, where the sun creates pools of light. Number five does a brisk trade in plants in a cottagey garden set round a small pool, with plenty of soft gold stone. A more modern garden across the road is filled with bright annuals, smooth lawns, paddling pools and children. Next door swathes of shrubbery and informal lawn produce a textured effect with a selection of rarities. Down the drive to number eight, a real gardener's garden in front of a beautiful house set off by the clipped yews and roses in the Monk's Way, a simple pattern of formal beds, grass, old walls and beautifully designed planting. Number nine, another garden with a pool at its heart, renowned for vegetables, cut flowers, hospitality and generosity. Last of all, a small cottage where an enthusiast produces more flowers than seems possible in the limited space: all beautifully proportioned and never crowded. A few yards down Church Hill and a much needed cup of tea.

The flower garden

My garden is primarily a plantsman's garden of flowering shrubs and herbaceous plants, with bedding-plants such as tender or half-hardy fuchsias, geraniums and annuals filling in odd spaces. Among the latter, antirrhinums, asters, tagetes, French marigolds and of course annual lobelias predominate. In addition, the lovely satin finish of the richly coloured trumpets of *Salpiglossus* does add that special look. For the fine summer evenings there can be no better scent than that of nicotiana: the variety Lime-green is a favourite with us, and it can be highly recommended as something different for flower arrangers.

Most gardeners find labelling a perennial problem. Ink wears off, and the labels seem to migrate or disappear altogether. In my experience an HB pencil provides reasonably permanent labelling, but I think that birds must be the main culprits in spiriting the labels away. How often have we all bought something really special, then after planting it dies down and the label vanishes?

Flowering shrubs really do give value for money. They only need periodic pruning to keep them within bounds, and the sprinkling of a slow-release fertilizer like bone meal in the spring. Just now *Viburnum plicatum* (Lanarth) is almost at its best and should continue for most of July. The layered effect of the flowering branches is so attractive. The lilac *Syringa X josiflexa* Bellicent is not seen as often as it should be; it is one of the hybrids produced by Isabella Pearson, a Canadian, and its darker pointed foliage and semi-erect panicles of rose-pink fragrant flowers are most distinctive.

In a small garden there is always a temptation to put plants too close together, for we underestimate their size when they are mature. The result is often something approaching a jungle. I make this mistake especially with flowering shrubs, and find the easiest way to control them is to prune carefully after flowering, so as to retain the bush's natural form. This can be done by thinning out some of the older parts, and thus letting in more light. Some plants, like buddleia and *Lavatera arborea*, the tree mallow, flower on new wood, and they can be kept to a manageable size by pruning hard to about 6 inches from the ground in late spring. Even so, the new branches may be 6 feet long before they flower in July. Sadly, I find that I have lost one of the witch hazels – *Hamamelis intermedia* Arnold Promise – for no apparent reason. It flowered well in the late winter, but as the leaves started to appear in May they just shrivelled up. Since it is a named variety, it was probably grafted on to a root-stock of *H. virginiana*, and the graft has failed. If shoots emerge from below ground, I shall know for certain that this is the cause.

A number of my new plant acquisitions are beginning to flower for the first time this year, and appear to have settled well in the narrow borders of the rear paved area. There is the very dwarf trailing *Antirrhinum molle*; only about two inches high, it has pure white snapdragon flowers with silvery grey foliage, and looks well beside *Codonopsis clematidea*, whose pointed, ovate, light-green leaves provide a beautiful background for the white, blue-veined bell-like flowers. But the real attraction of this flower is the delicate gold-and-deep-purple marking on the inside of the flower. It is common across Asia, and only grows about ten to twelve inches high, in a sunny, well-drained site. Another low-growing plant is *Cyananthus lobatus*, whose funnel-shaped, bright blue flowers are not dissimilar to those of the gentians.

Blooming for the first time are a collection of miniature roses, which I understand will require little in the way of pruning. They are scattered through the paved-area border, and complement the variety of leaf form and colour of the other plants. In the front garden, most of the trees now carry a climber, to bring some additional interest. The latest addition is *Tropaeolium tuberosum* Ken Aslet, planted to grow up the Kurile larch, *larix gmelinii*, var. *japonica*. The distinctive red-and-yellow spurred flowers on red stems are impressive, especially against the soft green foliage of this variety of larch. It will need protection after it dies down in the autumn, as the tubers are not hardy, so I will probably lift some of them as a safety measure. This is in contrast to *T. speciosum*, growing in our yew tree, which reappears happily every spring and is spreading far and wide.

This year the window boxes have been filled with a mixture of heliotrope and white and blue petunias, with a scattering of red and white antirrhinums edged with cascade lobelia. The hanging baskets each have a trailing fuchsia as the centrepiece: I am using Swingtime, La Campanella, Eva Boerg, Marinka and Harry Gray. The other planting is of petunias in various colours, the silver helichrysum, fibrous-rooted begonias, impatiens and cascade lobelia. By the end of July there should be a riot of colour – weather permitting. I have tried growing the delicate *Campanula cashmeriana* in a small hanging pot, and it is now a mass of cascading, powdery blue bell-flowers. It is a worthwhile plant to grow, and although not hardy it produces masses of seeds which germinate very readily.

The edge of the drive is particularly colourful at present with a variety of helianthemums or rock roses. As *H. nummularium*, it has a yellow flower and is native to the thin dry soils of limestone areas such as the Mendips and Derbyshire; but the garden varieties derived from it are not so fussy, provided their position is well drained and in the sun. They get very straggly if left for several years, and should be cut back hard as soon as flowering has finished. This is a good time to propagate new plants, and I will be taking cuttings from non-flowering side shoots. They are best taken by tearing them off, so that a small heel of the main stem is attached to the cutting. They will root readily in pots containing an equal mixture of peat and sharp sand, placed out of direct sunlight at midday.

In May and early June the main task was planning and planting the area at the rear of the house, which we increased in size by about 75 per cent, and gave a new boundary wall. Our contractor slotted edging pieces into a large area of concrete and filled this enclosed part, to a depth of about four inches, with pink Shap granite chippings. The rest of the garden has been laid with grey and red concrete flags simulating riven stone, and a big border has been made along the boundary wall. We had two fine shrub specimens – one *Wisteria sinensis*, the other a pyracantha – which formerly grew against the old boundary wall but were now left isolated. Both have been pruned into free-standing pillars. The wisteria is tied to an eight-foot post, and has been much admired, as it produces a cascade of mauve flowers. The pyracantha, too, in full flower, is equally attractive.

A large trough of alpines, together with various specimen plants in pots, stands on the area of granite chippings; they include *Ulmus elegantissima* Jacqueline Hillier, a very appealing dwarf elm which, even after ten years, is only 14 inches high. Unfortunately it is prone to scale insect, and I find the only way to combat that is by removing each one with finger and thumb. I hope my troughs of large tuberous begonias, which are just beginning to come into flower, will add another splash of colour to this garden, and give a Mediterranean effect, enhanced by the white house and boundary walls. This area is sheltered and faces south-west, so it should be a wonderful place to sit and enjoy the sunshine.

We are very fond of clematis and now have quite a large collection on the new wall – Nelly Moser, with large striped petals, is at its best now; Rouge Cardinale, a deep burgundy, is just breaking bud and will flower for two months at least. Later in July *C. jackmannii superba* will be covered in large, dark-purple flowers, which will contrast with *C. viticella* Madame Julia Correvon's small, wine-red flowers and those of a specimen of summer-flowering Jasmine, *J. officinale*, which came originally from my wife's home in Norfolk. In the corner, between *C. cirrhosa* Wisley Cream and *C. viticella*, a *Ceanothus thyrsiflorus* has just finished flowering. It is a new form, named Italian Skies, which is as good a description of the colour as could be.

The flag irises look like producing a fine show shortly, but I must take them up after flowering this year and divide the rhizomes, as the clumps are getting too large. Predictably the labels have long since disappeared, and we know them only by their colour. In recent times lupins appear to have fallen out of favour, but last year I raised some seedlings from one of the recently introduced new strains. The flower spikes are most promising, and a definite improvement on the old Russell strain. The form is good, and they are standing up well without staking. It certainly pays to experiment with something new each year. I only hope that they are not affected by the enormous grey-green aphids that attacked the old varieties two or three years ago. There were armies of them, and as fast as we sprayed them with every-thing from derris to washing-up liquid they remobilized and attacked again with increased vigour. It seems that northern aphids, like the people, are a tough breed.

Since the front drive consists of loose limestone chippings, we are always forewarned of visitors by the crunch of their feet. Windblown seeds and those dropped by birds germinate under the chippings, and by the time the seedlings reach the surface of the drive they are quite well established. Recently I have had a blitz on them, and in addition to removing the ubiquitous dandelions, groundsel and grasses, I have been able to relocate, or give away, a variety of plants: in fact, the drive has been nearly as good as a garden centre.

The kitchen garden

My kitchen garden, being about 100 yards from the house, tends to be forgotten except when produce is required. The apples have set well, and I think it will be advisable to thin out some of the clusters of young fruit, to lessen the weight on the branches and also to ensure good-sized fruit at harvest time. There is plenty of growth, and in a week or two I will be carrying out the summer pruning, which is a most important exercise: it is a major factor in triggering off the production of future fruit buds. Alas, in spite of all my efforts, the two pear cordons have again set no fruit and will be dug up shortly. This is also a good time to cut back to five leaves the new growth on the gooseberries and red- and white currants. In the autumn, they will need another cut to three. Not only does this encourage fruit-bud growth, it helps to remove aphids and any other nasties which are gathering in the growing tips.

All the cabbages are well established, and the cabbage root fly has affected only a very few of the Brussels sprouts, so we are looking forward to a good supply through winter to the early spring. Spring cabbage seed will be sown in the next few days, to produce good sturdy plants for putting out in early September. Having grown the variety Durham Early for many years, I'm using Flower of Spring this time, for no other reason than that I feel like a change.

Experts always recommend that we should plant only seed potatoes from certified stock, grown in Scotland or Northern Ireland. The main reasons for this are, first, that potatoes are hosts to at least 15 viruses in northern Europe, and, second, that many plant viruses are carried by aphids which are less frequent in northern Britain. Most of these viruses do not affect the edibility of potatoes, but they may, if you use the same stock over a number of years, lead to a reduction in the size of the crop as a result of the build-up of the virus in the potato.

The leaves of garlic and shallots are beginning to change colour. They will be lifted in early August, and I hope will dry off thoroughly in the sun before being stored. The shallots I planted in late November show a tendency to develop seed heads, especially the red variety Santé.

I have made a late sowing of turnips, and of lettuce for use in September. The spring cabbage sown at the same time has germinated well. So have the wallflowers, and they will be ready for planting out in the village-hall beds with the daffodils in late September.

After a lull in our own vegetable production, it is good to be enjoying courgettes and spinach beet, but because of the late sowing of the peas and beans it will be a few weeks yet before we can enjoy those.

At last I have tackled the job of lowering the hornbeam hedge that borders part of one side of the kitchen garden, alongside a sunken lane leading to some parish grazing-land. The hedge had begun to get out of hand, and at nearly 9 feet high it was excluding the light. After cutting the side, I took some 3 feet off the top, and managed to get this respectably level – not an easy job when using a saw and heavy secateurs.

The summer surfeit of vegetables and soft-fruit continues, creating the annual crisis in the kitchen because the freezer is full. What did we do BF (before freezers)? My memory as a child is of endless sessions of jam-making and bottling, to say nothing of hours of slicing up runner beans for salting down in large crockpots for use during the winter.

My grandmother, who lived in a village near Stratford-upon-

Avon, frequently cut off by floods in wintertime, had a large garden with numerous fruit trees, mainly plums such as Victoria, Czar, Pershore Egg, and the wonderfully named Warwickshire Drooper. Her motto, 'waste not, want not', ruled her life in late summer: she bottled plums, and made plum jam, plum pickle, and plum wine. There were always dishes of plums to eat raw if you could dodge the wasps; and a plum pie, or stewed plums and custard, was the predictable sweet when we were children.

The strawberry Tantalon has done exceptionally well, and runners of this, and of Cambridge Favourite, are now potted up. They will remain attached to their parents until well rooted, and will be planted out in their permanent positions towards the end of August.

The greenhouse and cold frame

In the glasshouse the green peppers have been repotted into 8-inch pots and the fruit are beginning to swell quite quickly. Seeds of *Primula obconica*, *P. malacoides*, cineraria and schizanthus have all germinated, and I hope they will provide a colourful display through the winter months. Winter-flowering pansies have also germinated well, and will be used both in the window boxes along with dwarf bulbs, and in individual pots in the greenhouse. The streptocarpus are now in full bloom and, as with all pot plants that are growing well, need regular feeding to keep up continuous blooming. I have shaken off all the old soil from the cyclamen corms and repotted them in a well-drained soil-based compost.

Standing outside the greenhouse are a number of fuchsias which I am training as standard bushes. They are now about 4 feet high, and as they have grown all the buds and sideshoots have been pinched out. After another six inches the leading shoot will be pinched out to encourage the development of a bushy top for flowering next year. Gardeners must always be planning for the next six months, or even two years – most of them are eternal optimists.

General tasks

The aubretia that grows in the drystone retaining wall of the drive has finished flowering and must be cut back quite ruthlessly to encourage a good display next year. Another job to be tackled before any strong winds blow is staking tall herbaceous plants, such as the delphiniums, which are a magnificent sight just now. They are only about three years old, and came as unnamed plants from a well-known breeder in the south-west. It is a pity to let them fall about in the wind, although my borders are now so densely planted that everything seems to prop up everything else. Not quite: the peonies have flopped outwards, and the gladioli lean.

Visitors are admiring the scarlet flowers of the Chilean Flame Creeper (*Tropaeolum speciosum*) as it clothes the yew tree. It was difficult to start, but once established it spread and is now covering the drystone wall along the roadside. A seedling has appeared some 15 feet from the parent, and is proceeding to cover the Japanese larch. Before long we will have red colouring everywhere and I am digging up pieces to pot-up and sell at a charity plant sale.

Whilst it is wonderful to have a long, dry, and warm summer, it does bring with it a number of problems we could do without. Problem number one: should we or shouldn't we water? I prefer to let most plants cope as best they can, for an essential part of gardening is knowing your plants and siting them according to their needs. For example, it is courting disaster to plant primulas, most of which are moisture- and shade-loving, in a sandy soil that dries out quickly and is in full sun for most of the day; but heathers, which are tolerant of quite excessive amounts of moisture, will also survive long periods of drought because of the waxy nature of their leaf surfaces, and their woody habitat. If I am forced to plant out members of the cabbage family in dry weather, I water them liberally for a few days, and then leave them; and they soon settle down, even if they do look a bit limp in the evenings. Leeks also need to be well watered at planting; but marrows and courgettes, as well as runner beans, need daily watering in dry weather.

Problem number two is that a long spell of hot, dry weather seems to encourage pests such as black-, white- and greenfly to breed at an even greater rate than usual. Last year my broad beans were pest-free, even without pinching out the growing tip when they were 3 feet high. Since I was growing a variety new to me, Witkiem Manita, I hoped I'd found a variety which blackfly did not like. Alas, it is not so, for this year I've discovered a severe infestation on two or three plants. Pansies and violas are prone to infestation by what appears to be a small brown fly, and if this is not dealt with quickly it will spoil the flowers completely.

Quite often the infestations can be the result of poor management: many of the common weeds are the hosts of these predators and, alas, we all have weeds in our gardens. The main culprits harbouring the pests – groundsel, thistle, nettle (both annual and perennial) and chickweed – do need to be kept in check; and sadly, over the years, I have concluded that there is no real alternative to hand weeding. Continually moving the surface of the soil by hoeing is a helpful addition, as it discourages the germination of unwanted seeds and gives the added benefit of producing a mulch of loose, dry soil, which helps to retain the moisture lower down. Spraying is often necessary in order to supplement the good husbandry, but I do try to be sparing in its use. I am sure that the widespread use of pesticides is a big mistake, for not only are the pests killed, but the natural predators such as ladybirds are killed as well.

Drystone walls always look attractive, whether they are made of the warm Jurassic limestone that occurs from the Cotswolds through to the North Riding of Yorkshire; or the older grey carboniferous limestones of the Mendips, Derbyshire and the Pennines; or the gritstones and sandstones of the West Riding – to mention but a few. They reflect the ancient and patient craft of choosing exactly the right piece of stone for a particular place, and ensuring that the wall will stand without any attention for at least 100 years. In the garden they also look very attractive as the edging to a raised bed, so it is unfortunate that they offer snug homes to so many garden predators, including mice, snails and slugs. In the last few days snails have ruined my hostas, mice have dined off young carrots and beetroot plants, and slugs have eaten the tender stems of the bedding annuals.

Another pest during June and July is the larva of the sawfly. Adult flies are small and inconspicuous (only 10–15 mm long) but the larvae are larger, being anything up to 40 mm. About 400 different species are known in northern Europe. They attack both wild and cultivated plants, but the majority only eat one type, or even one species. Almost all the larvae have voracious appetites, and can quickly strip a plant of its leaves. They overwinter in the ground around the plants, hatch out in the spring to the fly stage, and on the underside of the new leaves lay eggs that hatch out and repeat the whole process all over again. They are best dealt with by spraying with a malathion-based insecticide as soon as they are seen.

July

Planning ahead

Recently a garden journalist expressed the view that too much attention is given today to flowers which may be in bloom for not much more than six weeks of the year, and not enough to foliage which is there for at least six months. This set me thinking, and I have been taking a look at my borders and beds to see how far I have been influenced by the blooms when purchasing plants in flower at a garden centre. Most of us sometimes indulge in impulse purchasing at garden centres, caught by the attractive colours of massed blooms; but perhaps we should ask ourselves how the plants and shrubs will look without their flowers. It is worth recalling some words of Gertrude Jekyll, one of the greatest influences on gardening this century, and written nearly 100 years ago: 'The essence of a traditional herbaceous border is not so much a profusion of colours as a profusion of forms.' She also wrote: 'It can never be repeated too often that where some kind of beauty is aimed at, the very best effects are made by the simplest means. A confused and crowded composition is a fault in any picture.'

We should perhaps look at plants as skeletons clothed with leaves, and position them so as to provide contrasts and complements of shape and foliage. The flowers then become a wonderful bonus. For example, the pale yellow-green foliage of *Choisya ternata* Sun Dance is a joy in itself, so I am not too worried that it has not yet bloomed, though the white, scented flowerheads will be most welcome in due course. The grouping of this shrub with the large, mid-green, lanceolate leaves of the blue poppy, *Meconopsis sheldonii*, and the dark green ovate lanceolat leaves of bergamot, *Monarda didyma*, provides attractive contrasts in leaf shape and colour, and also in plant skeleton. Of course,

103

colour associations are very important in the garden, either as contrasts or as linked tones of a single colour, and were used not only by Gertrude Jekyll but by Vita Sackville-West in the gardens of Sissinghurst Castle in Kent. I planted a very dark pansy, Black King, at the foot of a tall bergamot, Croftways Pink; the pansy has grown up about two feet into the bergamot, and will provide an attractive colour contrast later. Meanwhile, the pansy flowers are adding colour to the bergamot stems.

I am thinking about taking softwood cuttings of some of the shrubs, for it is always useful to have replacements available in case of loss, or to give away, or for a future plant sale. Lavender is always a favourite. I grow four varieties: the dwarf *Lavendula angustifolia* Hidcote, so useful for the front of the border; the pink *L. intermedia* Jean Davis, which is also relatively dwarf; *L. stoechas*, the French lavender, whose flower spikes terminate in a tuft of purple bracts; and *L. dentata*, which also has a flower spike terminating in a tuft of bracts, but with deeply serrated leaves as well. Contrary to what the reference books say, I have not found this species to be reliably frost-hardy, so I grow it in a pot which is brought into the greenhouse for the winter.

The fuchsia cuttings have all struck, and will be potted up shortly to provide strong plants for overwintering and a good display next year. Various *Begonia rex* varieties have been split, and will be available for presents and plant stalls.

We are always told that it is not worth keeping seed to sow another year, yet the price of seed is high and packets often contain far more than we require for one year. So I have done some experiments with seeds, using some that were three or four years old.

I sowed both new and old seed on the same day, and in the same plot. All the new seed germinated within the limits required by the Seed Act of 1926; but the old seed was variable. The parsnips were appalling: only about 10 per cent germinated. Carrots were only a little better, at 30 per cent. So it is obviously not worth keeping these members of the Umbelliferae family to use another year. On the other hand, the germination-rate of old seed of peas and beans was about 75 per cent, and that of cabbages, cauliflowers, Brussels sprouts, and other members of the Cruciferae family such as lettuce, was well over 90 per cent, so there is some point in keeping surplus seed of these plants, provided you keep it in a dry and frost-free place.

Flower for the month: Alcea Hollyhock

In all the galaxy of saints one of the least regarded heroes must be St Joseph; except perhaps in Mexico, where he is remembered in a charming myth. It is told that one day God gathered together all the saints so that He could choose who should be awarded the honour of becoming the spouse of Our Lady. Wearying of the proceedings Joseph, who, as we know, 'was an old man', stuck his wooden staff into the ground, where, as he rested on it, it was transformed into a stem of flowering hollyhock.

Flowers for the house

In midsummer all the medium-sized annuals come into their own: snapdragons, asters, stocks and clarkia in the red/blue/pink range, and all the daisy flowered golds and yellows of rudbeckia, gaillardia, gazania, and marguerites. In the garden it is the time to grow a profuse jumble of colours which can be pleasantly echoed indoors when the weather is warm and the doors and windows are open. Mixed bowls can hardly contain too much colour, though my own preference is more subdued. On a hot day a tall narrow glass of grass, ox-eye daisies and dandelion clocks is peaceful and cool. It is necessary to pick clocks on a still day, but a quick squirt of hair spray will settle them safely.

Semi-wild flowers like foxgloves combine beautifully with swaying seed heads of different grasses, with perhaps a few pale blue scabious, chive flowers and francoa.

Lavatera is a useful cut flower, lasting well, but must be hurried to water after cutting, and at close quarters in the house it is possible to appreciate fully the intricate veining on the petals.

Hydrangeas look important clustered together but can be a nuisance if one head dies, and it is difficult to find a replacement of the correct size and colour.

Flowers for the church

Fortunate the parish which enhances, and shares, the beauties of its church in a summer flower festival. This can be an opportunity to spread Christian teaching, if the overall theme is didactic; an occasion for really studying one's parish church; and a time for a group of like-minded people to pool their common skill with flowers in the creation of a complete and harmonious design.

July is a month when many stately flowers, which show so well in large arrangements required in church, are at their best. Huge heads of pink, blue, purple or white hydrangeas make solid patches of colour; straight stiff stems of gladioli stand up well and are long lasting; and most rewarding of all, the first garden lilies, the queen of all flowers, used in Christian symbolism for hundreds of years. These gracious aristocrats are produced in an increasingly wide range of colours and are among the most amenable blooms to arrange.

The children's garden – *A Shrubbery*

If there is a very large garden around the house where you live it is quite possible that you might be allowed, for your own, a piece of land large enough for a shrubbery, or boscage. This could become your own private place where you could go when you wish to be quiet. Once the ground is prepared and a shrubbery planted it needs very little attention: some deadheading, trimming away old wood, and pruning into shape, usually after flowering, and that is all. You should enjoy consulting a gardening book about when to prune, as well as about what you can grow. If your space is small do not despair, plant fuchsias, miniature roses and lavender. For a larger space the list is endless: azalea for perfume; buddleias for butterflies; acer or cotinus for their special leaves; choisya and potentilla for masses of flowers; yellow broom or purple hebes.

Once your plants are established, go back to your book and find out how to take cuttings. Many shrubs 'strike' easily, and it is great happiness to give a present you have grown yourself.

Things to enjoy

- Passing by the soft-fruit beds and snatching a handful of raspberries or strawberries to eat, warm from the bush, in the sun.

- Listening to the bees, and being glad you remembered to plant shrubs which they will enjoy.

- Taking time off to enjoy picnics, either in the country or in your own garden; even the smallest town gardens usually manage a table and two chairs. Think of chilled wine, or home-made lemonade, and strawberries after a hot day in the city.

- A buddleia bush covered with butterflies. Try visiting a butterfly farm.

- Lying in bed listening to the soft whisper of summer rain and savouring the fragrance of the refreshed garden.

August

If you have two loaves, sell one and buy a lily.

August is the month for scissors: constant deadheading encourages new growth, but is also the quickest way of keeping everything tidy. Indeed, if there is heavy summer rain some quite severe pruning may be necessary to prevent damage to flowering shrubs, which may already be pulled down by the weight of blossom. Apply secateurs to a syringa drooping beneath the weight of fabulously scented, water-laden flowers, and the branches spring back into shape with the relief of a dowager shedding her corsets.

As the first flush of roses fades, except, of course, for those great performers the ground cover roses, ramping up the fruit cage and lying in mounds of profuse tiny flowers, it is a relief to have sweet peas. Grown for me every year by a friend, who chips, soaks and cossets them the previous autumn, they always tend to make a tentative start – followed by lavish growth with long flowerless stems, but once established, what joy! It is difficult to decide whether their early problems are due to bud drop or bullfinches. Equally welcome are the tiny flowered perennial sweet peas in shades of blue and purple. For years I coveted the local nurseryman's double-white, heavily scented variety. His exemplary generosity enhanced many weddings, where they made perfect pew end decorations, but sell a plant? No! Eventually the gift of a handful of seed offered hope: those I planted failed; those I gave to a friend, who planted them in individual egg shells, flourished, and one lot, in a small envelope, turned up on the alms dish at Holy Communion. Having been blessed one hopes they came to fruition.

A useful addition to the herbaceous border is a range of alliums: all carry their flowerheads on straight stems, and having no foliage they take up little space, growing between more leafy plants and contributing splodges of colour. Particularly attractive are the seed heads of the large-headed varieties, such as *A. Bulgaricum* and *A. Rosenbachianum*, which become a mass of spikey stars like arrested fireworks.

By August the earlier soft-fruits – rhubarb, gooseberries, strawberries, raspberries, loganberries and currants, black, white and red – should all be safely harvested: in practice there are usually some late ripeners, as well as plums and blackberries still to come. Strawberries are tedious to pick on a hot day, however carefully contrived the protective netting; but how wise were our Saxon ancestors who included 'strawberries' in their plant lists because they were, and are, delicious and attractive, and because a cut berry rubbed gently on the afflicted area relieves sunburn. Loganberries are hazardous, their long, whippy branches can easily pin an unwary picker to the churchyard fence. Other fruits are relatively trouble-free: the advice of an elderly cleric is to pick blackcurrants sitting comfortably in the kitchen. Since pruning entails cutting back the branches which have fruited, it is quick and easy to take an armful of branches into the house. Redcurrants perversely ripen first at ground level, but with the sun lighting them they are indeed the jewels of the garden: gleaming red fairies' earrings. Every year one currant bush in the vicarage garden mystifies visitors: crawl among the branches as you will, it really seems to produce red, white and black berries on the same bush. It is a very old bush and probably the object of some quirky grafting.

With such a prolific choice of fruit this is the month for that most delectable stimulator of generations of clergy, Summer Pudding, alias Parson's Buck-up.

If the weather in August satisfies expectations it is the most languorously balmy time of the year, and however much work waits to be done, it is an ungrateful person who cannot take time to potter drowsily around and say, with Beatrix Potter's Timmy Willie, '… you should see my garden and the flowers – roses and pinks and pansies – no noise except the birds and the bees …'

Competitions

Recently I have been judging some of the small towns for the 'Cumbria in Bloom' competition and, as usual, have been very impressed by what can be achieved with very little outlay. The competition does help to encourage community spirit and pride in the appearance of the town or village. Even in an area of high unemployment, the hanging boxes and window boxes overflowing with flowers somehow make things seem better.

In the last few days our village has been delighted to have been judged the best-kept small village in Cumbria. This follows closely on winning the small-village section of the 'Cumbria in Bloom' competition, and also the Eden Plaque for the best district entry. The judges' comment that Great Strickland was noted for its excellent garden standards was well deserved.

The flower garden

Summer is the time for roses, and none more excellent than the ramblers and climbers. Albertine on my pergola arch is a riot of coppery-salmon flowers, and lives up to one catalogue description as a 'wonderful sight in June and July'. The three new roses on the boundary trellis, the long-lasting dark-red Crimson Cascade, the yellow free-flowering Golden Showers, and the striking Joseph's Coat have settled down and are in flower, giving a foretaste of future displays when they reach the top of their eight-foot-high trellis support.

Some think that the increasing amount of black spot disease on rose leaves is due to a cleaner atmosphere and a reduction in the amount of sulphurous pollution. I'm not sure about that, but I certainly have more infected plants than I used to have, and our atmosphere has a fairly low level of pollution, especially in summer when fires are not lit. The fact remains that the new roses are spot free, so the growers are not to blame. It is only after two, three or more years that plants become infected, which seems to suggest other causes. In my experience, fungicidal sprays do little to control it, and I suspect that humidity may be the important factor.

The summer gives a grand opportunity for those who enjoy using scissors or secateurs, for there is a great satisfaction to be gained from using them, either for a sense of power, or simply in an effort to tidy up. There is no doubt that deadheading annuals and perennial border plants does extend the flowering season, and also helps to maintain a high standard of blooms, because the plants' energy is channelled into flower production and not, as nature intended, into seed production.

This is especially true of violas and pansies, which I like to see massed, but in a single variety. Two which I am growing for the first time this year, and which I can thoroughly recommend, are Rippling Waters, whose very distinctive flowers are dark purple with a white edge to the petals, and an F2 hybrid named Padparadja, which has exceptionally bright and intense orange blooms. I don't know its origin, but apparently it is named after a precious stone found in Sri Lanka.

The fibrous-rooted begonias have been a great success; it is the first time that I have grown them. The seed germinated well and they were easy to bring on; and although they were somewhat fiddly to deal with in the early stages, they certainly provide a vivid splash of colour edging the lawn. For sheer beauty and grace, however, the tall willow gentian *G. asclepiadea* is hard to beat. I must move mine, though, to a more moist spot, because they are only about 12 inches high instead of the normal 18–24 inches. No border should be without some members of the Allium or onion family. My drumsticks are in full bloom and are much loved by the bees. The heads of tightly packed dark mauve flowers are well named.

One of the problems of many spring- or early summer-flowering trees is that once they are over there is little of interest for the remainder of the year. To improve this I have established among them a number of later flowering climbers. In September to October the *Laburnum fossii* will support a mass of fragrant pale-yellow tubular flowers of *Clematis rehderiana*. *Clematis tangutica* adorns a flowering cherry, and just now the brilliant red flowers of the perennial nasturtium, *Tropaelium speciosum*, are resplendent against the dark green foliage of a small clipped yew.

Now is the season when wind can do a lot of damage because of the large areas of leaf surface. Tall plants growing in borders are affected much more than those in island beds, but in small gardens most of us have to be content with borders. Staking can be hidden if done early, so that the later growth hides it.

The hot, dry weather seems set for the foreseeable future, with only relatively minor fluctuations in temperature. The predominant bright green of landscape and garden is disappearing, to be replaced by an all-over brownness. The lawn has not been mown for nearly three weeks because of the lack of growth, and the number of large and totally bare patches suggests that there are places where very little soil covers the discarded stone and builders' rubbish from the restoration work on the house 25 years ago. I shall investigate some of these patches during the winter months, first carefully removing the turf and stacking it for replacement, and then digging. The last time I removed a piece of lawn, it yielded some 30 barrow-loads of rubbish from just half a metre under the surface.

Summer is coming to an end, yet all is not gloom. Some plants positively thrive on drought. The mesembryanthemums have been a lovely sight with their strident colours. The ground-hugging little alpine *Pratia pedunculata* from south-east Australia and New Zealand has been a mass of pale-blue star-like flowers, and *Lilium regale* has really been true to its name. This clump has been set off well against a backcloth consisting of the variegated leaves from *Stransvaesia davidiana*, the deep purple *Buddleia davidii* Black Knight, and a blue-green conifer whose label is regrettably lost. The new *Phlox paniculata* varieties have settled in well, and have produced good heads of flowers.

It is good to find that the torrential thunderstorms of late July did not do as much damage as might have been expected. The ground was fairly well dried out, so the rain was most welcome because it has penetrated well. This means that some jobs like lifting and dividing the flag irises, which had been deferred, can now be carried out, and the new plants settled in before the cold weather.

The kitchen garden

This summer, with the exception of raspberries, the soft-fruit has been excellent. Now the old wood of the blackcurrants must be cut out and each plant reduced to about seven or eight strong shoots for next year's crop. Ben Sarek and Ben More do well here, as they flower later and so tend to avoid the forest at pollination time. The gooseberries and red- and white currants, which I grow as double cordons, must be pruned back to about three leaves from the main stem. There appears to be a massive crop of blackberries on my Ashton Cross. The cordon apples are very promising, except that Greensleeves has a bad attack of canker. I am going to cut out the cankerous main stem to about one foot above ground level and train up a new side-spur as a replacement. I hope this will succeed; if not, then I fear the tree must go.

Unfortunately the kitchen garden remained uncultivated and neglected for nearly 30 years, until I hacked down the jungle and began to bring it back into production, so there must be an ample supply of dormant seed still present. Having taken photographs of the garden both before we started and at various times since, I am pleasantly reminded of the effort that has gone into its present state.

I am delighted with the way in which the brassicas are coming on, largely due to covering them with horticultural fleece when planted out. It provides protection from cabbage white butterflies as well as aphids, and acts as a permeable membrane, letting through the rain yet providing a form of cloche cover.

As August proceeds the onions finish growing and start to ripen. It is often recommended that the tops of the plants should be bent over to hasten this process, but my experience is that if you do try to hasten the ripening process the keeping qualities are impaired, and they are more susceptible to fungus and mould. Since I started allowing them to ripen at their own pace I have had little rot, and the onions have kept through at least to the end of

May. I also find that both garlic and shallots are better for being left until the tops have started to die down before being lifted.

The greenhouse and cold frame

In the greenhouse the fuchsias, begonias and streptocarpus are doing well, and although it can be time-consuming it is important to remove the flowers as they die off. Dead flowers are a potential source of sustenance for spores of fungal diseases which are invariably present in the more humid atmosphere of a greenhouse. Plants, like animals, respond to feeding and whilst we are recommended to use this fertilizer or that I find that plants, like humans prefer a varied diet; after all, we'd all get bored living solely on a diet of fish and chips or even oysters. I find working to a three-week cycle produces the best results for me – week one, a diluted proprietory liquid feed, week two, a solution of dissolved fertilizer, and week three, a home-produced organic feed. A sack of old sheep droppings steeped in a barrel of water produces an excellent liquid fertilizer which is known as 'sock' in my native Warwickshire; it needs to be diluted to the appearance of weak tea.

I have had a problem with the *Streptocarpus*, which is suffering from the attacks of an insect which prefers to bore holes into the base of the tubular flowers to get at the nectar rather than come in directly from the top of the flower; presumably its proboscis is not long enough. This makes a real mess of the flowers. I am inclined to suspect a wasp-like fly recently seen lurking around a nearby cluster of *Papaver somniferum*, the opium poppy. A drug addict, perhaps?

This is a good time to take cuttings of plants which are either not hardy or, although apparently hardy, prone to disappear during the winter months. My technique is to prune the cutting to about 2–3 inches immediately below a node, and to strip off the leaves except for a cluster around the growing tip. This provides enough leaves to allow photosynthesis to carry on, while encouraging the other end to produce roots in a medium of half peat-based compost and half silver sand. I usually insert 5–6 cuttings round the edge of a 5-inch pot, having dipped them in a proprietary rooting compound, and then put the pot into a plastic bag tightly tied to keep the moisture in and to provide a suitable warm environment to encourage rapid root development. It is important not to forget to attach a label giving the name and the date. The pots are then left on a part of the greenhouse bench shaded from direct sunlight. Generally I find that rooting takes place within two to three weeks.

The soft-tissue cuttings taken so far are of argyranthemums (the modern name for marguerites) in variety, pentstemons, pansies and violas. Many of the latter do not come true from seed, so that such beauties as Rebecca, The Gambia, Molly Sanderson and Moonlight are best reproduced from cuttings. I've also taken cuttings from a variety of pinks, such as that old-fashioned double white Mrs Sinkins, with its delightfully heavy scent.

Of the hardwood plants which strike easily I take cuttings from a lovely deep red broom, rosemary and various lavenders: Hidcote, the pink Jean Davies, and the French lavender, *L. stoechas*. Another beautiful lavender, but needing winter protection because it is not frost-hardy, is *L. dentatus*, with its distinctive tooth-like leaves and a flower not dissimilar to *L. stoechas*. It is a lovely plant for a heated conservatory. I have a big potted stock plant which lives outside from June until the first frosts, and is then brought into the greenhouse for the winter; cuttings are struck from this to give to friends.

General tasks

In the gardens growth has been strong and sturdy, especially of the weeds. Weeds such as groundsel, shepherd's purse and chickweed are not the only self-seeding enemies. A close check needs to be kept on some of the border perennials by 'dead-heading' regularly.

There is much tidying up to be done as the dry weather continues. Many of the border perennials that finish flowering early, like the clumps of aquilegia, astrantia, campanula, peony, meconopsis and delphinium, can be cut down to about six inches above soil level. Since most of my borders are mixed, cutting down withered plants makes more room for those that are coming into bloom; and as it is really a garden for all seasons it is always in need of attention. At the same time, the cuttings provide fodder for composting. I am sometimes asked by those who rate their artistic prowess somewhat higher than mine: 'What is your philosophy for planting?' Being a plantsman rather than a designer, I reply: 'I plant where there is space.' To me, the challenge is not the painting of a picture with plants, but rather that of getting some beautiful rarity to thrive and bloom in the conditions I can offer.

Flower for the month: Lily

For centuries white lilies have been considered a symbol of purity, frequently associated with Our Lady. At a time when few could read, much emphasis was placed on didactic symbolism in paintings, carving, embroidery and stained glass. Early painters included lilies in portrayals of the Annunciation, and Dutch flower painters devised arrangements of lilies, irises and other of the Virgin's flowers. Still used in 20th-century decoration, especially at Easter, ancient church and monastery gardeners cultivated lilies for the great liturgical festivals.

A 13th-century archbishop instructed an abbess to build a new garden gate for, he explained, '… these lilies we believe to be the ornaments of virginal purity, which by reason of certain matters found in our visitation lately, we desire to protect'.

The lily has also become the emblem of St Catherine, who, attempting to convert her pagan father, the Emperor Costis, succeeded when she demonstrated that faith could miraculously imbue the formerly scentless lily with the pervasively sweet fragrance with which we associate it today.

Flowers for the house

August is the month when summer becomes gently lethargic, and many of the delicate blues, pinks and mauves of high summer become a little wan. It is pleasant to anticipate the stronger tones of autumn and welcome the vibrant colour combinations of gladioli: gold, yellow, pink, magenta, purple, orange and even green. Spectacularly dramatic when massed in a huge container, they can be just as effective, as the lower florets fade, cut down and arranged in a spikey wheel, which, with oasis, is easy.

It is well worth growing ligularia in a damp corner. Both the common varieties have wonderful dark sherry-coloured leaves and stems, supporting glowing orange flowers.

It is possible to organize a series of lilies to flower from July to September, but care needs to be taken in ordering them if they are for cutting: as well as a wide variety of colours there is also a wide difference in stem lengths. In addition, some lily perfume is so strong that only one or two stems are bearable in one room.

In gentler shaded flowers there should still be some tall blue, or white, campanulas, phlox, with their characteristic dry papery smell, and ceanothus, sporting the colour of either Oxford or Cambridge.

Flowers for the church

After the profusion of flowers in high summer, August brings a little restriction in the choice suitable for church, so one hopes for a few weddings to help out with the cost of florists' flowers. Having said that, it must be admitted that if the range of species is limited, colours are in breathtakingly profuse supply. Dahlias should be flowering now through September and into October.

A wise nurseryman used to let his church customers browse through his acre of dahlias with their own scissors, and of course he sold far more that way. Whatever bits of material brides produced to match up the flowers for church, those dahlias were sure to oblige with the desired shade. The rows were shoulder high by the end of August, and were stripped of blooms each evening, in wellingtons and a swimsuit if it had been raining.

Growing up the enclosing walls were hedges of double, white, perennial sweet peas, which, with a froth of gypsophila, took care of the pew-end containers.

The many churches dedicated to St Laurence celebrate the patronal festival, in the middle of the month, with a blaze of fiery red flowers. Red for a martyr and white for a saint – breathtakingly beautiful, but horror for brides with medical connections, wriggling to avoid some dire superstition connected with those colours.

At one St Laurence church, flowers were chosen to emphasize the two tones of the damask hangings: gladioli, dahlias and carnations in blood red and scarlet spiked with white.

The children's garden – *Miniature gardens*

Do you ever wonder what to do in the school holidays? A happy way to pass time outside, or in a shed if it is wet, is to design a garden. It need cost you nothing and requires no plants. Start with a box of damp compost: make it as small as you like, dolls' house size would be fine. Take tiny cuttings of small-leafed plants and stick them close together for a hedge; bare twigs would make a fence, and a trickle of fine gravel paths. An old saucer, or shallow tin, would do for a pool, with one or two pebbles in it and the edge masked with tiny bits of moss. Float some small flower heads as though they were water lilies; but do not use daisies, for they will fold up, go to sleep and drown. Flowering shrubs often have small flowers. If you are very nimble-fingered you could make steps up a hill with a tree on top, or a bench. Plant little flowers and leaves and water it very gently. If you keep it in a shady place it will last a day or two, and when it fades you just replant with different snippets.

Tailpiece

Conservation is now the fashion, but nevertheless it has to be managed, and must not be used as an excuse for doing nothing. One country churchyard I know has a large sign at a side entrance: *This part of the churchyard is a conservation area.* It had certainly been left for natural development, but so has the rest of the churchyard and the vicarage garden next door. On the other hand, I remember a churchyard in Norfolk where part is set aside, and a splendid noticeboard lists the plants which might be found there, together with their season of flowering, and also names the more important small mammals, insects and butterflies to be seen. Conservation at its best.

Things to enjoy

- The perfume of lilies.

- Watching for a field of ripe corn washed through with scarlet poppies, still to be seen in spite of pesticides; or even a rare crop of brilliant blue borage, an expensive requirement of the cosmetic trade.

- The full variety of English garden vegetables.

- Time spent usefully in the garden with a pair of scissors, deadheading and cutting back herbaceous plants to encourage side shoots.

September

*When the lamps in the house are lighted it is like the
flowering of lotus on a lake.*

So often September is both one of the warmest and most colourful months of the year in gardens. Nevertheless it is the first month of autumn, and it is always the change of 'feel' that marks the end of summer so decisively. The sweet pea stems fail to achieve any length; there is just a hint of brown in the leaves, and however balmy the midday sun there is a coolness. The first feeling of change usually comes among the blackberries, only a few fields from home: as the late afternoon light changes, the countryside smells strange, and in the sudden stillness lies a brooding lethargy, an expectancy, a suggestion of older gods.

Among September flowering plants are *Nicotiana Sylvestris* – these open with a dramatic flourish of trumpets, twenty or more four-inch white blooms flaring out from a four-foot stem. All very stately and exotic, but with just a touch of malevolence in the carnivorous appearance of the large, woolly leaves, sticky enough to become insects' graveyards. An appropriate, and slightly sinister, neighbour for some years was a datura, Grand Marnier, whose liqueur-coloured blooms resemble nicotiana, although the whole plant is larger. It was a challenge to nurture this showy plant in North Yorkshire as well as to survive its acquaintance, since all parts are seriously poisonous.

Some years ago I lost patience with a pomegranate, which heaped coals of fire on my head by sprouting a prodigious number of seedlings where it had been thrown away. Most of these were quickly sold at a plant sale: the one I kept made healthy growth for years, but never flowered; it probably needs company of another sex.

Another strange plant flowering this month is cleome which, like camels, seems to have been designed by a committee. A rather clownish plant, at first it seems to be a lupin, then it becomes stockier but with that part of the stem carrying flowers soon beginning to droop. The leaves offer two unpleasant surprises, being very sticky and carrying almost invisible thorns. The loose collections of oval pink or white petals, with long, dramatically curved stamens, look like nothing so much as pretty dancing crane flies.

Japanese toad lilies were supposed to contribute to the unusual corner, but always seem reluctant to grow at the same time as other plants, and so tend to get lost in the boscage. Their small mottled deep pink flowers are pretty enough whenever they can push past their neighbours.

If there has been a reasonable amount of rain, September offers a glorious show of colour: a second flowering of roses; many annuals still performing well; second helpings from herbaceous plants, if they were sensibly cut back after their first blow; and all the brilliant colours of dahlias, outdoor chrysanthemums, Michaelmas daisies and many others. One is reminded of a patch-work quilt: not a seamstress's showpiece, but a real cottage quilt, full of patches of colour, of materials given or exchanged, and full of reminders of the donors, or sources of origin.

Many years ago it was from cuttings from friends' gardens that we created a small sheltered private area. Very quickly about fifteen different Veronicas, planted round the top of a curved wall, with ground trailing species falling over, grew up into an inviting corner to lie on the grass, or play with babies or kittens, and it was an extra pleasure to be able to continue exchanging cuttings. It seems a pity, especially for a vicarage garden, that Veronica, a good Christian saint, should have become Hebe, the goddess who carries nectar.

Gardeners need to be exemplars of forward thinking. Wholesale catalogues come in, raising the usual expectations for next year: September is a time to begin thinking of next season and to formulate resolutions and hopes. One annual hope is that next year the local pigeons will find a more attractive social centre than the supports of the fruit netting. Really one prefers not to have a crisp white icing of bird droppings on the best raspberries.

Flower shows

Summer's end is the season of flower shows, when neighbour vies with neighbour to produce the largest marrow, the straightest runner bean, the most perfect sweet peas or the best pot plant. In Cumbria the vegetable-and-flower competition is usually part of a larger agricultural show, although some of the smaller villages have a simple flower show which also includes sections for cakes, scones and jam, together with one for children.

One year, in spite of the extended drought, the standard of exhibits was extremely high, and reflected great credit on all concerned. One or two gardeners in this area seem to win the open classes at most local shows; this is done by carefully working out how long it takes the plants to get from seedlings to maturity, and then working backwards from the show date to fix the sowing time.

We were recently on the Cheshire-Shropshire border, house-sitting while our daughter and her family were on holiday, and took the opportunity to revisit some gardens known to us, and to spend a day at the Shrewsbury Flower Show.

The gently sloping Shrewsbury Showground at The Dingle, situated in a loop of the River Severn, is one of the most beautiful in the country. The highlight of the show was the display of specialized vegetables by an old-established family firm with a national reputation. I am trying their new Brussels sprout F1 Stan, which won an Award of Merit from the Royal Horticultural Society in 1992. It is looking very promising alongside F1 Peer Gynt and Bedford Pillbasket, and with a long harvesting period from November to March it should be a winner. I shall report on its performance in due course.

Other trade stands which particularly attracted me were those with sweet peas, begonias and delphiniums, streptocarpus, roses, pansies, violas, and bulbs. The sweet pea is the one flower which I like to see cut, since the form and the shades of colour of the flowers on their stiff stems lend themselves to pretty arrangements. And there is the added bonus of their powerful scent. Begonias have an air of opulence, whether they are tenderly cosseted for exhibition with special wire supports for their heavy flowerheads, or grow, like mine, in troughs and tubs for a colourful display in a paved area.

No mixed border should be without at least one delphinium. At Shrewsbury we were particularly impressed by Royal Flush – a dusky pink with a white eye – and bought a plant. We obtained a few more streptocarpus for the greenhouse. The modern hybrids are very showy plants for a shaded greenhouse or for a windowsill that does not receive the full midday sun.

I also visited the Southport Flower Show. The showground in Victoria Park has been improved enormously in recent years, with brick pathways laid between the rows of trade stands, instead of gravel or ash. I was reminded by the number of stands selling bulbs – daffodils, tulips, snowdrops, crocuses and scillas – that bulb-planting is nearly here, for important as the competitive classes are in these big shows, I think most people go to see the magnificent trade exhibits by leading specialists. Looking at some of them, it was hard to realize that we were enduring a drought.

Visiting gardens

I have paid my first visit to the University of Liverpool Gardens at Ness, on the Wirral Peninsula. The sheer variety of the planting schemes, whether of herbaceous plants, alpines, or roses, is a joy in itself, but I found the extent of the shrub-planting even more impressive. Certainly it is a teaching laboratory for anyone inter-ested in or concerned with planting, especially if they live close to the sea. There is an excellent plant-sale area, and since I can never resist the temptation I came away with three penstemons to add to my collection. I also acquired some additions to the meconopsis that I have already, and I will follow the growth and development of two of these with interest. All the reference books list *M. wallichii* as a synonym for *M. napaulensis*; but I bought two plants, one labelled *M. wallichii*, the other *M. napaulensis*, and they differ in the development of the crown and the leaves, one being darker than the other. There is some similarity in the actual leaf form. Perhaps the flowers will turn out to be of differ-ent colours, the possible range being from shades of red through to blue with the occasional white. They will be monocarpic, and therefore will die soon after flowering, so the seeds must be collected. The other meconopsis purchased, *M. dwhojii*, which the label described as yellow, does not appear in any of my reference books, although it is listed in *The Plant Finder*. It represents impulse-buying at its worst: I found the name fascinating. The leaves of this plant are typically lobed, but are very much narrower than those of most meconopsis.

The flower garden

It is a pleasant surprise to find, as I did a few days ago, that the *Colchicum speciosum* is in flower, for these large naked pink crocus-like flowers seem to appear fully out overnight. I'm also delighted to see that two new plants acquired last autumn are now fully established and blooming. First is *Clematis rehderiana*, which has started to take over the laburnum, and is a mass of delicate little pale-yellow hanging bells which are fragrant and are said to have a scent similar to that of cowslips. The other is *Liriope muscari* – a relatively small plant with lanceolate leaves and mauve or lilac flowers resembling grape hyacinths.

Autumn is, of course, berry time; and whilst most are still inconspicuously green the berries of *Tropaeolum speciosum* are now turning to the bright purple which make them as conspicuous against the dark green background of the yew as were the flame-red flowers a month or so ago. The tall unidentified cotoneaster by the front gate is also turning colour and is enhanced by the variegated leaves of the honeysuckle *Lonicera* var. *aureo reticulata*, while the clusters of little berries on *Callicarpa giraldii* are turning to the bright violet colour that never fails to cause comment.

The wild fruit of the hedgerows – hips, haws, and crab-apples – are extremely brightly coloured this year, as well as prolific. I wonder whether nature is warning of a severe winter to come, for certainly the last few winters have been very mild. The wild sloes are ready to pick and appear to be of excellent quality: I shall soon be preparing to make sloe gin to my own recipe.

In the alpine garden the hardy cyclamen are giving a most attractive display. In particular *C. hederifolium* is now well established and is the earliest of my collection to flower. It is also the hardiest of them all; but it does not like a heavy clay soil – not surprising for a woodland plant. The smallest of all cyclamen, *C. intaminatum*, from south-west Turkey, is also in bloom, with flowers only about half the size of those of its nearest relative *C. cilicium*; and these are a very pale pink, and without the red base to the petals so common in most species.

With sunshine and a rise in temperature the autumn gentians should be in flower. The mid-to-late-summer flowering *G. septemfida* is over, as is its variety *G. lagodechiana*, which I think one of the most beautiful of all gentians because of the very deep blue of its trumpets. I have a sandstone trough filled with *G. sino-ornata*, *G. macaulayi*, and the delicate pale shades of the Inschriach hybrids, all of which are in bud and showing colour. Following on in the plunge bed is a pot of *G. sino-ornata*, var. Mary Lyle, which is pure white. It provides a lovely contrast when planted with the blue varieties, but most of these gentians, especially *sino-ornata*, are lime-haters, which is why they do well in the troughs here but not so well in the garden.

The Michaelmas daisies will soon be reminding us that autumn really has arrived. Although very prone to the disfiguring effect of mildew, there are some beautiful vibrant colours among the recent introductions. Among the *Aster nova belgiae* my favourites are Royal Ruby and the rich deep-pink Alma Potschke, neither of which needs staking. Especially valuable in the autumn border is *Aster lateriflorus horizontalis*, with its masses of small pinkish-white flowers borne on sturdy stems. It is very attractive to the bees and it is also long-flowering, developing a particularly handsome purplish foliage.

Among the less hardy plants providing a wealth of colour just now are the penstemons, which never fail to be admired by visitors. *Lobelia cardinalis* with its lovely dark burgundy-coloured leaves and red flowers which always come out late with me, and also the striking Cambridge-blue *Salvia patens* and *Cosmos atrosanguineus*, often called the chocolate cosmos from the perfume which it exudes. Now is the time to be taking cuttings of all these against the risk of losing them during the winter. The parents will be protected with straw and a good mulch of composted bark, and hopefully will come through unharmed yet again.

Already some trees, noticeably the acers, are beginning to show autumn tints, and, in some cases, to shed their leaves. A distinct variation in colour of the leaves of *Cercidophyllum japonicum* appears in early autumn: those on the new season's growth are dark coppery pink, whereas those on the old wood are bright green. This shrub makes a most distinctive feature of the garden. The leaves of the spindle, *Euonymus europacus*, are also beginning to turn a bright red, but no berries have developed, in spite of plenty of blossom in the spring on both my specimens. I think that help with pollination may be needed. As if the leaf-colour changes are not enough to tell us that autumn is with us, the swallows have been congregating in their hundreds on the electricity and telephone wires. I'm sure that within a few days they will be off on their long flight to North Africa, and, if their arrival marks the coming of summer, their departure marks its end.

General tasks

I am continuing to cut down the herbaceous plants as they

finish flowering, for not only does this make the borders and beds look tidy, but it helps the plants to conserve their strength and produce sturdy growth for next year. Very soon I will be moving those plants which I've noted are in the wrong places, and I will be dividing clumps that have become too large. Now is the time for me to tackle once again the perennial problem of hedge woundwort, *Stachys sylvatica*. I think we are now within an ace of eradicating its pernicious creeping roots. Small fragments of it, left in the ground, will quickly grow into strong new plants.

Flower for the month: *Colchicum Autumnale* – Autumn Crocus

In the Song of Solomon, saffron is among a list of precious species bidden to flow forth. It is not surprising that this derivative of Autumn Crocus, sometimes called Meadow Saffron, is still expensive today since it takes some 60,000 stigma to manufacture one pound of dye. In ancient Greece, brides were said to wear the 'bridal saffron' and in Persia, saffron was used to dye the king's shoes.

Most people today find the strong aromatic perfume too power-ful; in a less personal-hygiene-conscious age it was highly favoured for use in theatres and at banquets.

The plant is unfortunately wholly poisonous (perhaps one should use it carefully in the kitchen!), so that farmers have destroyed the native crops and a field of gleaming mauve crocuses, flowering after their strappy leaves have died, is a rare sight. Bereft of leaves they look strangely undressed which explains their local names of Naked Ladies or Strip Jack Naked. The French name is altogether less delicate.

Flowers for the house

The first month of autumn offers all sorts of ideas for the house. The leaves are changing colour and make arrangements complete in themselves, especially if they are placed where the sun can light them up. Except for love-in-a-mist, whose spikey seed heads in a froth of 'mist' are as pretty as their flowers, most blooms in the garden are in much more robust tones. Long gone are the pastel shades of high summer. Many flowering shrubs are worth searching for a second flowering: Mexican Orange, with its rosettes of shiny light leaves, seems to manage clusters of white flowers in most months; fuchsia, disappointingly short-lived in water; blue abelia; some hebes and hydrangeas, are all in season. Cosmos, which first flowers in August, seems to relish cooler days and by September can be reaching six feet. Pretty as is the most common *C. Bipinnatus* it is well worth growing some of the more unusual shell, picotee or striped varieties, for it is only in the house that they are seen close enough to appreciate their intricate markings. Unfortunately they are not much use in church, as after cutting they need to be rushed to deep water.

Flowers for the church

Although there are plenty of flowers in September sufficiently tall and robust to use in church, it is not the most exciting month. Gladioli and dahlias make a welcome change from pastel shades in August, but as both are susceptible to water damage they can be disappointing in the wet of September, only to stage a revival in early October. Chrysanthemums are plentiful, but as they will be the backbone of church flowers for the next two months it is as well to hold back if possible.

Tall fronds of yellow-flowered feathery fennel give the necessary height to a church arrangement, but need care in placement as they can disappear into the background. Equally tall, and with stronger colour, are the tassels of golden rod, which soon spreads to a mini-forest in the garden if not well disciplined. Chinese lanterns actually display better in church than in a house or garden: the bright orange lanterns lurk under the leaves and are only seen to full advantage from slightly below, as in a tall pedestal vase. Once welcomed to a garden, they will crawl everywhere and produce lanterns to light up many a display.

If bright flowers are being used it is well worth considering seed heads to mix with them. Favourites must be alliums, great clusters of spikey stars, or for bulk and subtle colours, great heads of hydrangea, which seem to dry themselves on the bush and last for months.

The children's garden – *A shade garden*

Some plants prefer living in a damp place away from the sun. For instance, there are many different varieties of fern, which are not too difficult to find; Solomon's Seal, sometimes called false frankincense; bluebells; lilies of the valley – be careful they do not hide themselves completely – wild arum lilies, which have many names such as Jack-in-the-pulpit; sweet smelling bergamot; papery astrantia; golden kingcups; all sorts of hostas; and a pretty plant with pink and green leaves which smell of tangerines. Nearly all shade plants have specially interesting leaves: if your mother is a keen flower arranger she will be delighted if you are able to give her leaves, or flowers, which you have grown; or perhaps you could practise flower arranging yourself.

Tailpiece

Another of this year's successes has been the reintroduced old-fashioned sweet pea Matucana, which has fully lived up to expectations, and has attracted much interest and excitement. I will certainly include this in next year's seed order.

My greatest joys, which I have done little to earn except to wait patiently, are the abundant blossoming of *Eucryphia nymanensis*, and the anticipated blooming of *E. glutinosa* for the first time. It is now also a mass of firm, plump buds. Over the last few years, I have been tempted to conclude that the eucryphias would not succeed in this garden, but have received such encouragement that I have tried to exercise patience.

Things to enjoy

• Wandering round your garden with a handful of delicious dessert gooseberries, sweet and juicy.

• On a country walk looking for fungi, colourful umbrellas for fairies; useful additions to cookery and a variety of bizarre shapes and smells.

- Eating your own tomatoes, warm with sun and full of flavour.

- Cooler evenings and the gradual colouring of leaves until everywhere there is gold and red and russet and orange.

- Picking blackberries in the country, and making jams, jellies and pickles.

- Early chrysanthemums with their easily identifiable bitter smell.

October

A halo round the moon is a sign of wind.

Delightful it may be to reflect on Keats' gentle autumn vision of mellow fruitfulness, but in our north-east corner they may still be struggling with late harvests; and far from becoming 'close bosom friend of the maturing sun', October only brings us the sun as a fleeting visitor. In most parishes this is the time for Harvest Festivals, pulpit swapping and the subsequent mell suppers – mell being a Norse word meaning meal, and can Yorkshire folk enjoy their food after hard work! Harvest decorating is a happy abandonment for flower decorators, but misery for vergers who clean up. Permissiveness is rife: any and all colours are acceptable, everyone brings their own flora, with oddments of fauna, and to the resulting garish blaze of colour are added vegetables, fruit, sheaves, grapes and bread for the altar, and just about anything eatable. The rest of Saturday is spent clearing up the mess; everyone sings their heart out on Sunday; and on Monday it is all dismantled, and taken to the sick, bereaved and housebound, and the church is cleaned up all over again.

This is a good time of year to enjoy a plant sale: how often do we deplore nature's prodigality as we split up perennials, thin out seedlings, and throw away healthy plants for lack of space. What to one gardener is an unwanted nuisance will be a plant worth paying for to someone else. Looking at boxes of expensive physalis berries, imported from Bolivia, it seems ridiculous to suffer the scratches necessary to root them out from among the miniature rose patch, where their orange lanterns clash with the soft pink and white roses. Perhaps they are worthy of more respect since I am assured that the crème de la crème of society enjoy these bitter-sweet fruits, coated with pink sugar, and with the papery calyces twisted into butterflies' wings.

Among the largest trees in Scalby churchyard are several horse chestnuts. I had always supposed that their name derived from the facsimiles of horseshoes – complete with the correct seven nail marks – which scar the twigs wherever a leaf has fallen. Not so: long before the Turks were shoeing their horses they were using an infusion of chestnut bark to treat equine strains. Now pharmacists are researching the aescin content of conkers to ascertain its value in human medicine.

Alongside the chestnuts grow several whitebeams, aesthetically satisfying all the year round, the early soft silvery-green leaves a perfect foil to dark yew; the loose umbels of creamy flowers are sweetly scented, and the red fruits, pomes, are gobbled up by the blackbirds and starlings, which ensures a supply of sturdy seedlings. A dictionary will tell you that a pome is 'a priest's hand-warming ball of hot water'. I know one priest who has survived a long ministry with never a pome in his cassock pocket, but perhaps one could try a clerical outfitter for a pome pocket. An unexpected whitebeam bonus is that the leaves, a simple shape, with very pronounced veins, make excellent patterns for chocolate leaves.

Chocolate cosmos is a plant worth persevering with, both for its stylish growth and elegant cup-shaped flowers poised on long slender stems. On a dull day these flowers really are the colour of dark chocolate, but when the sun is out they are suffused with the deepest glowing red, and the perfume is of the most expensive bitter chocolate, at least from the distance of a bee's nose.

As autumn progresses the bees are brought down from the heather moors for their winter rest, which they have surely earned. One is left amazed at the performance of these industrious little creatures: from the local honey farm bees collect nectar from the borage fields and, calculating the length of a bee as about one inch, the journey from hive to borage and home is about equivalent to a Spitfire doing Heathrow-Edinburgh-London, and that is far from one journey a day, and with a fully laden return flight.

Visiting gardens

Recently I visited an outpost of the Royal Botanic Garden, Edinburgh: the Younger Botanic Gardens at Benmore, just north of Dunoon on the Cowal Peninsula of Argyllshire. I was struck by several tall (30–40 foot) slender trees covered in masses of white flowers, which proved to be the finest specimens of *Eucryphia glutinosa* I have ever seen. They thrive here because the microclimate of the valley of the River Eachaig, which flows through the 220 acres of the gardens, is fairly mild, and the valley is sheltered. *Eucryphia glutinosa* in its native South America prefers a sheltered, sunny position and a moist, lime-free soil. Recently I was shown a specimen of *E. glutinosa* in the Howgill Fells area, which had only a few flowers. For various reasons, this shrub had been cut back quite severely. I am fairly certain that this was the reason for its lack of bloom, and that it will recover. The reason for the poor development of my own specimen is that my garden is far from sheltered, and there is rather more than a hint of lime in the soil; but I shall persist, trying the effect of more shelter, and peat at the roots.

The flower garden

Not for nothing do North Americans refer to the autumn as the fall, and on our village green the *Acer*, or maple, is busy shedding its dark golden leaves to produce a lovely colourful carpet. In the garden the leaves of the common spindle, *Euonymus europaeus*, have now turned a brilliant red. I planted it about four years ago, and as yet the white late-spring flowers have failed to set to produce the characteristic rose-red seed capsules. I am especially proud of an *Acer palmatum*, which is now about four feet tall. Its pale yellow tints provide just the right background for the striking violet berries of *Callicarpa giraldii*. The new *Acer palmatum dissectum atropurpureum* has settled in well, but will need some protection this coming winter as these trees tend to be half-hardy until well established.

Although we may have a natural desire to clear away all dead stalks, foliage and flowerheads, there are advantages for the birds in not proceeding too quickly. During the last few months a pair of collar doves have made their home with us; they do not appear to have done any damage to tender shoots, but spend a lot of time pecking around and eating seed heads – and certainly, since a pair of thrushes arrived, we have had fewer snails and slugs than in the past. Whilst having lunch last week we were visited by a cock pheasant, which quite fearlessly poked around the *Chaenomeles speciosa*, eating the pips of the quince and nibbling the seed heads of *salpiglossus* and antirrhinums with obvious enjoyment. We enjoyed the visit too.

The kitchen garden

Overall, the kitchen garden has been a great success this year, in spite of a very late spring when the soil was not in a fit state for sowing seeds. Although they were not planted until the end of March, the garlic cloves are now of a very respectable size, and the Golden Gourmet shallots have averaged 1½ to 2 inches across, with very few going to seed. My wife has been using these in lieu of onions. The brassicas have also been good. The cauliflower Igloo produced large, well-protected heads that developed quickly; it has done better than Dok Elgon. The cabbage Hispi also performed well, as did the Calabrese Corvet F1.

The autumn cabbage Stonehead F1 has produced compact, almost spherical, balls which are reputed to stand well without splitting, so we hope to use them through to early December, when the purple-tinged and flat-headed January King will be ready. This year I have tried a new red cabbage, Red Winner F1, which is looking very promising too.

However, my greatest success has been the runner bean Liberty: from a short double row of 24 plants we must have picked around 15kg, with very few beans being less than 12 inches in length. They had a good layer of manure beneath them, and have been watered regularly from the greenhouse waterbutt.

Summer finished quite sharply at the end of the third week of August, when the temperature dropped significantly and the rain became more frequent. Those who normally stir before daybreak indulged in a little one-up-manship by reporting hoar frost on the fields, which disappeared miraculously at first light. Whether this was true or not, field mushrooms, which seemed to be fairly abundant, quite suddenly became scarce and, almost as if they knew that autumn was upon us, the blackberry (Ashton Cross), the Victoria plum and the greengage rapidly ripened. Fortunately we got the plums and greengages picked before the wasps had made too much of a mess of them, and even the damson managed 20 fruits – this after 14 years. Having ignored our dire warnings in the past, it will be felled as soon as the leaves have fallen.

General tasks

I am making a start with pruning the shrubs and small trees now that they are more or less permanent fixtures. Ideally they should have been planted so that they had room to develop into their proper form, but most of us have to prune our shrubs to keep them under control. Many people are scared of pruning because they think that they'll do it at the wrong time, will remove too much, or that the shrub they cherish will never recover from their well-intentioned ministrations. I have found that, if a few simple rules are followed, the chances of failure are minimal compared with those of success. Do try to keep the shrub as near to its natural shape as possible – pruning is not about hedge-trimming or topiary. Many of the best-known shrubs are spring- or early-summer flowering, and pruning them after they flower encour-ages new growth on which flowers will appear two years hence. Most of the late-flowering shrubs bloom on the new season's wood and should be pruned in the following spring. These shrubs include *Buddleia davidii* varieties, fuchsias, lavatera and hydrangea. In general, evergreen shrubs, such as *Berberis darwinii*, escallonia and *Lonicera nitida*, which are often used for hedging purposes, will tolerate severe pruning, even to the point of being cut down to ground level. On the subject of how much to remove, I advise erring on the side of caution, remembering that if you do not take off enough wood you always have a chance to take more later. I am to remove about one-fifth of the old wood, remembering that the harder a shrub is pruned the stronger and more vigorous will be the resultant new growth; and I prefer to start pruning early in the life of a shrub so that it becomes used to a fairly light annual prune. There are some shrubs, however, that require only minimal pruning, whatever size they ultimately reach, because they often do not start their flowering life until they are mature. *Eucryphia glutinosa*, some of the viburnums, daphne and corylopsis are of this type.

As plants die down for the winter it is very important to either label them or at least mark the site with sticks, for nothing is worse than digging over the borders or preparing the ground to plant a new acquisition, only to dig up a clump of something which has died down leaving no trace in the winter months, such as *Incarvillia*, *Colchicum*, lilies or Crown Imperials.

The lawn is not only completely recovered from the almost lethal application of Jeyes Fluid in the spring, but there is no sign of any return of moss. To encourage the tight thick sward to recover its full strength from the summer of mowing, a dose of autumn lawn fertilizer, which is richer in potash, can be applied, although it may still be necessary to give a few more mowings, depending on how warm November is.

Planning ahead

I am planning to plant up the window boxes with dwarf tulips and winter-flowering pansies again. The tulips are all varieties derived from the species *T. kaufmanniana*, or the waterlily tulip, whose main characteristic is flowers about 3–4 inches in length, usually in two shades of colour. My selection is literary and musical: Shakespeare, salmon-red flushed with scarlet and a yellow base; Johann Strauss, white with a red base; and Gluck, red with a white base. For winter colour indoors, a few bowls of hyacinths will spend the next eight weeks under the spare bed, together with some small bulbs. This year I have chosen *Puschkinia libanotica* – a small hardy bulb native to Asia Minor and the area eastwards. Related to the scillas, it looks rather like a dwarf blue hyacinth.

I have been saving my own seed from some of the herbaceous perennials. It is reasonably easy to do this, provided the seed is dry. If the seed is not absolutely ripe the seed heads can be put into a paper bag to finish the ripening process in the house. Plastic bags should never be used because moisture cannot escape from them, and so mildew will attack and destroy the seed. It is not worth one's while saving seed from annuals as they rarely come true: their production is a specialist operation, much of it done overseas in a warmer climate.

Flower for the month: *Dipsacus Fullonum* – Teasel

At the season of Harvest Festivals it seems appropriate to consider the teasel, a plant which like most harvest gifts is both decorative and useful, though brave is the floral artist who handles it. It prefers to seed itself as near to footpaths as possible where its vicious prickles can rip the arms of passers-by. Rearing their purple heads crowned with great dignity, they enjoy a proud history of service in the cloth trade and are still in demand for some specialist fulling tasks today. Anyone familiar with the London guilds will recognize three teasel heads on the arms of the cloth workers.

For medicinal purposes only the root is used which Dioscorides recommends for vanquishing 'warts and wens', or for bathing sore eyes. Warts and wens being less common now, it is still worth trying an application to abolish freckles, to which many gardeners are prone.

The cupped leaves can hold several wine glasses of rain water, earning the plant the names Venus' Basins or Shepherds' Cups.

Flowers for the house

October could be called the golden month, or even the month of golden daisies: flower arrangers are spoilt for choice, and all the characteristic golds of autumn flowers are complemented by glowing colours of leaves. Most months produce some daisy-shaped flowers, in seasonal colours, but October brings a wealth of taller, more robust blooms, in a wonderful range of yellow, gold and bronze. Heleniums; gaillardia; rudbeckia; coreopsis; gazanias, with their coiled caterpillar centres; and chrysanthemums – all blend with either autumn foliage, or with dried seed heads.

For a room which really demands pink shades there are still single chrysanthemums; echinacea, cone flowers with strong hairy stems and pronounced brown centres; and all the glowing purples and pinks, tempered with white, of asters, either the simple single daisies, or the untidy, tousled heads of the doubles. Tobacco plants usually flower on into November, but their attractive, softer purples and pinks can become a trifle overpowered in a large room. A full bunch of the green variety is more eye-catching.

Flowers for the church

For most churches October is the month to celebrate Harvest Festival, that most relaxed thanksgiving, when any decoration is acceptable, however messy. Unless the weather has been disastrous, dahlias should still be available. One northern nursery-man used to cut his dahlia beds to a manageable height with a chainsaw, so that by October they were once more in full bloom and as jungle-like as in August. Outdoor chrysanthemums and Michaelmas daisies are both flowering and tall, and strong enough to raise the height of arrangements well above sheaves of corn, vicarage marrows, mountains of vegetables, apples every-where, and all the gift baskets of goodies traditionally destined for the sick, bereaved and house-bound.

Most churches hide away some dinosaurs of containers to drag out for Harvest to support pampas plumes, sprays of elderberries, blackberries (sure to fall off as the devil has spat on them by October), hips, haws, and flame-coloured creepers. All the strident autumn colours of gold, magenta, scarlet, purple and flame – as many shades as Joseph's 'amazing technicolored dreamcoat' – create a regal tapestry in a dark church or a patch-work of brilliance in a light one.

The children's garden – *Town garden*

Even town houses with no garden usually have somewhere where it is possible to grow a few flowers. Boxes on windowsills, or balconies, baskets hanging beside the door, or suspended at different heights up the wall, containers fixed to railings or on a below-pavement area, or up the sides of steps, can all be used to make a colourful display. They will need good drainage – some broken crockery or small stones covering the holes in the base – some watering and some feeding with a sprinkling of general fertilizer. None of this takes much time and the result is rewarding.

Spring bulbs such as hyacinths, crocus and daffodils do well in containers, but choose short-stemmed varieties as they may lean towards the light. Baskets can be filled with trailing summer annuals to cascade down the wall. Petunias, lobelia, nemesias, verbena, geraniums and nasturtiums are all suitable, and can be matched in ground-level containers with similar but non-trailing plants. Pansies have a long flowering period and you could try growing variegated ivy, clematis, honeysuckle or climbing roses up the wall or along the railings.

Tailpiece

A suburban fox broke into my sister-in-law's garden shed in Nottingham earlier in the year, and dragged a bag of bone meal across the lawn, spilling a trail behind him. The result is a similar trial of luxuriant dark-green grass, as a consequence of the slow release of phosphorus, potassium and calcium. Perhaps on another visit he could be persuaded to spread the bone meal more evenly.

Things to enjoy

- Leaves. Sweeping them up for leaf mould; walking through drifts of crisp leaves on the village street, or in a country lane; and the appetite resulting from this vigorous activity.

- Bonfires, the smell, the swirling white smoke and the sense of achievement in so much tidying up.

- Putting away the mowing machine, clean, and in good repair, of course.

- A second good growth of herbs if the weather is kindly, before their final cut back in November. If your kitchen is tall enough, hang some up to dry.

- A country walk to collect inspiration for Harvest Festival.

- The full glory of the hunters' moon on a clear night.

November

One joy scatters a hundred griefs.

(Macmillan Treasury)

The Indian summer, which seemed to be going on for ever, ended in a flurry of heavy rain, high winds and severe frosts. Not only did the autumn continue wet and windy, but we have had the first snow. It was only about an inch, which lasted a few hours, but the Lakeland fell-tops and the Pennines were well covered. This cold snap, with hard frosts at night, has hastened the fall of leaves and finished off the dahlias and any geraniums that had not been lifted.

The rain has helped to make the ground rather plastic, so that with the strong winds those shrubs and trees still in leaf have tended to rock where staking was inadequate. The damson tree in the kitchen garden was blown over at a 45-degree angle because the fencing-post stake had snapped. Although the tree is about ten years old it has always tended to rock, but now it is secured to a stout six-foot oak post with the addition of a supporting truss. It is always a good idea to check stakes and ties regularly to avoid damage to well-loved plants. I've just had to resecure the 'tree ivy', *Hedera helix erecta*. It is now about three feet high, roughly fan-shaped, so the leaves present a large surface area to the wind. It will probably be a good idea to lift it after the March gales, and replant more deeply. The wind has also blown off parts of the Michaelmas daisies, which have only just finished flowering; but with next year's shoots and plenty of root attached I am potting these up for one of my plant sales next year.

157

Visiting gardens

I thoroughly recommend a visit to the Lakeland Horticultural Society's gardens at Holehird, near Windermere.

The Holehird estate was developed by a Manchester industrialist, John Dunlop, in the last three decades of the 19th century. For the first half of this century the Grove family, generous benefactors to the area, developed and expanded the gardens, as well as advancing horticulture by helping to sponsor the plant-hunting expedition of Reginald Farrer and William Purdom to Kansu Province of north-west China in 1914–15. It was on this expedition that plants which we regard as quite common in our gardens – *Buddleia alternifolia*, *Viburnum farreri*, *Clematis tangutica*, *C. macropetala* and *Gentiana farreri* – were collected. As with many other notable gardens, Holehird suffered from neglect during the Second World War, but when the Lakeland Horticultural Society was founded in 1969, members took on the herculean task of clearing the overgrown gardens, extending to some 12 acres.

Today Holehird is a Lake District star attraction, with all the work of maintaining the gardens, plant propagation, and so on, done voluntarily by members. Visit Holehird and enjoy not only the superb displays – which include the walled garden (mainly herbaceous), the alpine garden, and the national collections of astilbe, hydrangea and polystichum ferns – but the views, southwards across Windermere, and the peace of these hillside gardens alongside Holehird Mansion (which is now a Cheshire Home).

The flower garden

The last two days have been dry and much warmer, so I hope to make some progress with cutting down the herbaceous plants, dividing the Michaelmas daisies, phlox, gaillardias, coreopsis, and the beardless irises such as sibirica and chrysographes. Quite a large area of one border will need to be dug over completely.

It is obviously autumn in the garden with a wonderful range of red, bronze and orange colours of the falling foliage of acers, amelanchia and cercidophyllum. There is also the spindle, and the lovely little flowering cherry, *Prunus incisa Kojo-no-mai*, a variety of the Fuji cherry well known for its brilliant autumn colour, which looks well as a pot plant on the rear patio.

In contrast, the roses have taken on a new lease of life and are full of bloom again, as is *Eucryphia nymanensis*. Strangely, the first frosts of September did not affect the fibrous-rooted bedding begonias which, in the window boxes and other containers, are now 12–18 inches high and full of flowers.

The dahlias were well and truly black after their first hard frost and are now waiting to be taken up, along with the gladioli. They will be well washed and then soaked in a fungicide mixture for about half an hour, dried thoroughly, and stored in a frost-free place until spring, the dahlias probably under the spare bedroom bed, and the gladioli in the garage.

The various half-hardy salvias were also blackened and must now be cut down, lifted and boxed up to be placed in a frost-free place. The frost has also cut down the perennial flame nasturtium, *Tropaeolum speciosum*, but the underground tuberous roots are hardy, and next spring the new growth will once again spread out over the yew tree, extending their territory to take in neighbouring shrubs and small trees. I don't really mind this take-over, because of the eye-catching scene that results.

Care must be taken, though, of the newly planted *Tropaeolum tuberosum* var. Ken Aslet, which is only half-hardy and must be covered up. I see to my horror that this form, the most commonly grown in this country, has received attention from the taxonomists and is now to be known as *T. tuberosum* var. *lineamaculatum* Ken Aslet. I presume this means that the tubers are narrow and spotted, but I don't propose to dig mine up to find out.

The kitchen garden

Although one season may not be busier than another in the garden, it always seems to me that there is a greater sense of urgency during the autumn months, when unexpected frosts so often catch the unwary and spoil the last pickings of runner beans or damage the potatoes. This year I have been worried because my red onions just kept on growing and refused to show any signs of ripening; so at the end of October, before any really hard frosts occurred, I lifted them and laid them out on the greenhouse benches vacated by the tomatoes. Now both the tops and the roots are dying down and the onions are drying out in the gentle heat. Next year I must plant them earlier: they obviously need a longer growing season than the white onions. Now that one side of the kitchen garden is cleared of produce, I hope the weather of the next few weeks will allow me to get it manured and dug.

If good crops are to be produced it is most important that the soil is in good heart with a good tilth. I am fortunate in having a ready supply of free farmyard manure, together with a deep soil slightly on the heavy side, which means that it does not dry out too readily.

The weather seems to be against me: whenever I have a completely free day there is a howling gale or it is pouring with rain, yet it is always ideal for gardening when unavoidable commitments have to take priority. In spite of all this, I have taken down the netting covering the top of the fruit cage, assisted by my ten-year-old granddaughter, who is already a keen gardener and talking of taking up horticulture in due course. Last winter one of my neighbours left the covering netting on his fruit cage, and the consequent damage to the cage posts from six inches of snow was disastrous. It is easy to underestimate how quickly snow, especially wet snow, will settle on netting; and it has considerable weight.

Other tasks either done or in process of being done include staking the Brussels sprouts. Even though I had planted them deeply, most of the very heavy stems had keeled over, and the sprouts were being enjoyed by the slugs.

We have now tasted the first of the new potatoes planted in pots in July and then grown on in a plastic dustbin. The verdict is excellent; it is good to have real new potatoes in November and December. The celery this year has suffered from the summer's drought – after all, it is a bog plant – and the sticks, although of excellent flavour, are not as long as I would like. However, the Brussels sprouts are buttoning up well and look like producing a good crop, and if the top growth is any guide, the parsnips will be good too. The great thing about gardening is that for all the failures there is always compensation in the successes.

The pruning of the apples and pears is complete. There has been a good crop of apples this year, but too much damage from the codling moth, so very soon I will put sticky bands round the trunks of the cordons to stop the moths' movement up to the blossom and fruit. A few weeks before the blossom buds break, a spray of winter tar-oil wash will complete the treatment. The two pear cordons have always been a disappointment. This year the Conference bore only one pear, its first, but it was a beauty to eat; and I noticed when pruning that the other one, William's Bon

Chrétien, has a lot of fruit buds, so both these trees have been reprieved for another year.

The gooseberries and currants, both red and white, are full of buds, and the final pruning must be done soon to keep the cordon form in proper shape. I'm a believer in growing them this way because it is economical of space, yet gives a heavy crop. They are easier to pick, too. Unfortunately this method cannot be used for blackcurrants because they fruit on new wood. After picking nearly half a hundredweight of fruit from the one blackberry, and leaving behind at least another quarter of a hundredweight, I am going to reduce the number of shoots retained for fruiting next year. Nevertheless, I continue to recommend Ashton Cross as the best blackberry, not only for cropping but also for flavour – always supposing you do not mind the very thorny habit.

The greenhouse and cold frame

The new cold frames have arrived from the joiner – four double Dutch light units; and all the rooted hardy and half-hardy plants are safely under protection, which can be increased by covering the glass of the frames with sacking or old carpet. In due course I aim to increase this protection by fixing bubble film to the interior side walls, a technique I've seen used to great effect at Holehird.

There is much to be done in the main greenhouse, since the appalling weather of the last two months has hampered the preparations for winter. All the contents need to be removed so that the glass can be washed down with Jeyes Fluid to disinfect, kill spores and discourage algae; the two-inch layer of Shap granite chippings on the stages needs to be well watered with Jeyes, too; and the insulating layer of bubble film for heat conservation must be put in place. Two dry days without frost and reasonably sunny are needed for all this, since the plants must be put outside.

The greenhouse is serving a number of purposes for a variety of plants, at present. The young plants of *Primula malacoides* and *Cyclamen persicum* are coming on well, and should be in bloom for Christmas. At the same time the late-summer-struck cuttings of fuchsias, which will be grown on through the winter, are making good sturdy plants. I am training some of them as standards, which are always useful for show purposes or as features in a bed of annuals. The divisions from the *Begonia rex* varieties are also shaping up well, and will be useful as presents or for a plant sale. Meanwhile tubers of the large-flowering begonias are also in the greenhouse, drying off. After three years they now are about five inches across, so next year I think I will cut them into sections.

All the tender or half-hardy herbaceous plants, such as *Lobelia cardinalis* and Queen Victoria, the salvias, *Cosmos atrosanguinea* and the rooted cuttings of several varieties of argyranthemum, calceolaria, and the deeply-divided-leafed lavender, *L. dentata*, are now in the plastic house and will be covered with fleece when the weather gets really cold. Greenhouses, even the unheated type, are very useful in winter as well as summer, houses for all seasons.

Planning ahead

I am still taking cuttings of some plants as I cut back the parents. Pentstemons and osteospermums are not always hardy: indeed, it is best to assume that they may not survive the winter; but there is plenty of suitable new growth on both these groups of herbaceous plants. I find it best to take short (three- to four-inch) stocky cuttings, remove all leaves from the part of the stem which will be in the potting compost, and dip the cut surface in a proprietary root-compound before putting five or six plant cuttings round the edge of a four- or five-inch pot filled with half peatbased compost and half silver sand. The latter can be partly or wholly replaced by either vermiculite or perlite. I then place the pot in a plastic bag secured with a tag and labelled with the plant's name and date. If the pots are placed on the greenhouse bench in a good light and a gentle heat, the cuttings should root in four or five weeks. It is important not to open the plastic bag until it is certain that the cuttings have rooted, i.e. when the top appears to be growing. Of course, it is equally possible to strike the cuttings on the windowsill of the kitchen or bathroom, provided that the light is good and the temperature reasonably constant.

Some of my tender border plants must be dug up and put into boxes or pots for the winter in a frost-free place, preferably one where the temperature does not fall below 40F. The pelargoniums have been taken out of the window boxes, cut right back and put into boxes. They have had a dose of fungicide and will be kept relatively dry until growth starts again next spring, when they will need to be potted up and grown on. *Cosmos atrosanguineus*, the deep maroon chocolate-scented cosmos, on the other hand, will die down and, having a tuber like a dahlia, is best potted up and kept just moist until new shoots start to appear through the soil, when proper watering should start again.

I usually buy my bulbs for the window boxes at an auction in early November. This year, for an outlay of about £30, I got 90 dwarf tulips, red, yellow, and red-and-yellow-striped; 50 mixed hyacinths; 175 narcissi (Barrett Browning, Scarlet Gem, Geranium, and Yellow Cheerfulness); as well as 60 dwarf daffodils in six varieties for the rockery. This I think is a fair bargain, and they will come to no harm through being planted a little later than the books recommend.

Plant for the month: *Equisetum* – Mare's Tail

One of the oldest plants in the world, and one of the least loved, its remote ancestors flourished with the dinosaurs, and its former gigantic size, and grotesque appearance, well matched those extinct monsters.

In an informative churchyard conversation the first sexton spoke of horse's tail; the verger called it bishop's tail; while the gravedigger correctly named it *equisetum*, and told us that the roots of this almost indestructible menace grow deeper than a treble grave, becoming blacker as they lengthen. He only hinted at the horrid superstitions attached to this ancient weed. The second sexton contributed his recipe for their annihilation – mix up a porage of sodium chlorate and paraffin, then, when the plant is in vigorous growth, take a handful and stroke it up the length of each stem.

Flowers for the house

To provide flowers for the house in November, without help from a florist, greenhouse, or conservatory, can be something of a challenge, though not impossible. There is nearly always 'the last rose of summer' happy to be rescued from the cold, and for these a glass specimen vase is ideal. Sprays of magenta winter savory make a reliable standby: their wiry curved stems will support frailer flowers, and the tiny dark green leaves are a foil for pansies, violas or snippets of late rockery flowers. Our medieval ancestors relished savory as a culinary herb, but to most modern palates it is unacceptably pungent and better used solely for decoration. There is scarcely a month when mahonia, hebe, or one of the viburnums do not produce something decorative.

At least in the north, where spring comes slowly and autumn is often mild, it is not unusual to find pockets of late clematis in flower. These arrange beautifully, but need a little care. They should be carried in a flat basket to avoid petal damage, then their stems should be dipped for a moment or two in boiling water: they are then ready to be supported by their own leaves and seed heads in a flattish bowl where they will last quite well. It is possible, but avoidable, to scald them to death.

Flowers for the church

It must be admitted that there is really not very much to be found in most gardens in November with which to decorate a church: but the silver lining to that little cloud is that it is the time of year which one associates with handsome great chrysanthemums with their characteristic bitter smell. They are readily available at florists, and of all plant specializations in greenhouses and on allotments, cosseting competition-standard chrysanthemums must be one most widely practised. Few flowers show themselves off so well in church, and even if they must be bought the cost is not too prohibitive, since in a cool church they will last for several weeks.

Remembrance Sunday falls towards the middle of November, and for this white chrysanthemums are entirely suitable, contrasting with red poppies, either silk or Earl Haig. Clippings of bay tree, the laurel of the ancients' laurel crowns, or even bare twigs backing red, or red and white, flowers, make an effective statement.

The children's garden – *Bulbs and planting*

November is the time for all sorts of jobs before you leave your garden to its winter rest.

First of all, tidy up dead annuals, rake up leaves and any rubbish, and, if you have a herb garden, cut back all the perennial plants to ground level. They will bounce back next spring.

If you plan to plant a rose bush you should do so now. Make sure you dig a hole large enough to leave plenty of room for the roots to spread comfortably, firm the soil down well, and add some support if this seems necessary.

Many flowering shrubs may be planted this month, when their leaves have fallen.

Finish planting bulbs of spring flowers in the garden – daffodils, narcissi, crocuses and tulips. Any bulbs you want to flower indoors should already be in their pots in a dark place.

It is not too late to plant an amaryllis bulb to flower at Christmas as they only take 6–8 weeks from planting to flowering. These exciting plants carry several bold, bright trumpet-shaped flowers on long, stiff stems, and once in flower last for a long time.

Tailpiece

Garden centres always seem to be so full of tools, equipment and machinery for the garden that I sometimes wonder how they ever manage to sell them all. Manufacturers are always trying to boost their production by extending their ranges, by producing new designs, or simply by giving their products a built-in obsolescence. I fear this last is a fairly recent phenomenon connected with mass production and the throw-away mentality. I still use the stainless-steel spade and fork, given me by my father in 1940 at a cost of £5 each, when I rented my first allotment, and likewise the old draw hoe made by the village blacksmith, for which I make my own replacement blades from an old saw. The little roller I use for the lawn is at least 80 years old; it belonged to an old uncle of my mother's, and still has its cast-iron plate bearing the name of the retailer: R. Peters, 174 High Road, Wembley, London. I don't suppose the shop is still there, but I'd be interested to know if anyone remembers the shop. The roller has been looked after carefully, oiled and repainted; and although it lives outside it is good for at least another 80 years.

Things to enjoy

- Picking any flowers still in bloom. No one is going to sit out in November, so enjoy late-flowering roses indoors.

- Fiddling about packeting, and labelling, seed you have saved, which should be dry by now.

- The spine-tinglingly eery cries of hunting owls while you are warm in bed.

- Preparations for next year. This is the time to plant bulbs, in pots, or drifts under trees, or neat rows for cutting, or clustered in patches to make eye-catching pools of colour.

- Reminding yourself that there will be no more hedges to cut for some months.

- Doling out a prodigal feast of manure wherever it will be appreciated.

December

A book is like a garden carried in the pocket.

In the run-up to Christmas, the garden takes a back seat as far as priorities are concerned, and little work has been done in the past month. The lawn is continuing to grow, so I am glad that I managed to mow it on the second of two consecutive dry and windy days. The blades were set higher than the usual summer setting, so that the grass was not weakened, as this could result in damage if the weather should be severe this month or next. I cut the lawn edges too, so for a little while we really looked very smart. An application of moss-killer has checked the growth of moss in the lawn, and another application will be given, to complete the task.

I have just acquired a hollow-tined lawn aerator, a hand-operated piece of equipment which takes out small plugs of soil to a depth of about four inches. It is a rather laborious task, but it enables air to be introduced into the compacted lawn; a dressing of coarse sand then brushed over will help to improve the drainage, and so further discourage the growth of moss. A strong garden fork can, of course, be used to aerate the ground, and can be quite effective; but it obviously does not do as good a job as the aerator because it does not actually remove any soil.

Many gardeners who pride themselves on their lawns get very upset at the appearance of worm casts. This is a pity, I feel,

173

because worms do enormous good in helping to aerate the soil and prevent its becoming too compacted by frequent mowing and treading. The old-fashioned besom brush is ideal for scattering the casts and at the same time providing a light top dressing. The active presence of worms also indicates that the soil is in good heart.

Well-berried holly has been prolific this year, and there was plenty available for decorating as well as an adequate supply for the birds. So we were disappointed and somewhat put out to find that they not only devoured the scraps we put on the bird table, plus nuts and coconut, but also stripped a holly wreath at the front door of all its berries. They certainly prefer holly berries to those of the pyracantha, which they invariably attack last of all, leaving an untidy mass of short berry stems. Before the spell of icy weather over Christmas there was still a touch of colour in the garden, but the frosts finished that. Only the winter heathers are pushing flower stems through the snow. Now we look forward to the bright yellow inflorescences of the hamamelis or witch hazel to say that spring is on the way.

In some winters berried holly seems to be in fairly short supply, owing to the failure of the female flowers to set their fruit. In common with most fruit-producing plants, holly seems to have good years and poor years, for a variety of reasons.

The flower garden

As I walked round the garden a few days ago I found the superb white clematis Marie Boisselot still in flower two months after it should have finished blooming; and the Kaffir lily, *Schizostylis coccinea*, is starting to flower again. The lovely bright red spikes of this plant related to the gladiolus must be thinking they are back in their native South Africa. Although I personally have never had the space to spare, it is said that the flowering season of *Schizostylis* can be extended well into December by growing it in the greenhouse at a temperature of about 8–10C. Nearby in the flowerbed the dwarf red-hot poker *Kniphofia*, Little Maid, which only grows about 18 inches high, has thrown up its characteristic creamy white spikes again after flowering in September, making a real summer picture. In a sheltered spot a large clump of *Astrantia major* var. Shaggy has extended its flowering from August, much to my wife's delight, for its long flower-like bracts make it useful for flower arranging.

I never seem able to get the Christmas Rose, *Helleborus niger*, to bloom at Christmas. This year again there is no sign whatever of buds. Perhaps I should try putting some glass protection over the plants earlier in the autumn. *Helleborus foetidus*, however, is beginning to show signs of developing the massive panicles of pale yellow-green flowers tinged with red which are such an impressive sight around Easter-time. The only problem I find with this plant is the degree of self-seeding. In fact, it's almost as bad as groundsel.

A very good-value plant, once it is established, is *Erysimum* Bowles Mauve, which is closely related to the wallflowers, but does not set seed, so has to be propagated from cuttings. Those I took in early November are looking well and may be ready to put into individual pots and be plunged in the cold frame before Christmas. The value of Bowles Mauve lies in its apparent ability to be more or less perpetual flowering; and although most author-ities suggest that erysimums are dwarfs, i.e. about 18 inches high, Bowles Mauve grows almost into a shrub three foot high and three across. It does appreciate shelter from the winter blast: I always take cuttings in the late summer or autumn, just in case I should lose the parent, and they are always good to give to friends or for plant sales.

There is still a bit of colour around from the autumn in the remaining berries, and the foliage of euphorbia. There are even signs of the forthcoming spring, as *Jasminum nudiflorum* is a mass of yellow on bare stems; and I notice that the snowdrops are beginning to push their shoots through the ground. This year for the first time the corkscrew hazel *Corylus avellana contorta* (Sir Harry Lauder's walking-stick) is producing a good show of catkins. Sadly I lost a *Garrya elliptica* last year, so we will miss the lovely long grey-green catkins early next year. It is not particularly hardy and needs some protection, certainly in its first few years. As mine was in a rather open position, I'm afraid it got caught by last winter's wind and frosts; but since it does not like its roots being disturbed, I could not win.

In contrast to the plants which have extended their flowering season, there are a lot of plants which are more advanced than I care to see before the end of the year. Not only is *Viburnum X bodnantense* in full bloom, but the buds of *V. X juddii* and *V. plicatum* Lanarth are beginning to swell quite rapidly. Before long I think I must give them some protection from frost, as I do not want them to flower before April. *Bodnantense* is no problem, as it is one of the hardiest of viburnums, as well as one of the earliest to flower, together with its parents *V. farreri* and *V. grandiflorum*, which grow wild in northern China and the Himalayas respectively.

In most years *Prunus subhirtella autumnalis* begins to show a few flowers in late November and then continues flowering like this right through to March or April, when it bursts into full bloom. It is now well into bloom and the delicate, spindly branches are a mass of small semi-double flowers, about half an inch across, white with a tinge of pink. It is going to give us much pleasure for the next few months, as it is clearly visible from the kitchen, sitting-room and our bedroom windows.

Sycopsis sinensis, the close relative of hamamelis (witch hazel), is in full bloom, and will stay like that till late January. The smallish yellow flowers with their prominent stamens are an attractive sight, as are the bright red berries of *Stransvaesia davidiana*, which provide a vivid contrast to its variegated leaves. Also causing comment are the violet berries of *Callicarpa giraldii*, which are very striking against the bare stems of the shrub.

Some years ago I acquired a seedling of *Eccromacarpus scaber*. According to the books, this native of Chile is only half-hardy in the British Isles and, except in the mildest areas, is cut to the ground by frost. I planted mine on the rear wall facing roughly south-west, and there it rapidly climbed the trellis to the roof of the house. Its orange-red tubular flowers provided a wonderful spread of colour against the white walls. Now, some 15 years on, it still survives, without any dieback, to give a good splash of colour from late May to October. It self-seeds readily, but seed I have collected invariably fails to germinate.

The greenhouse and cold frame

Recently I was lucky to have a sunny and comparatively warm Saturday, and so was able to empty the greenhouse to get the bubble film fitted. Unfortunately I was not able to wash down with Jeyes Fluid, so I will have to keep a keen eye for aphids, especially whitefly, as well as red spider mite. I must also clean the clay pots frequently with one of the algae-killers, to control the growth of green slime.

General tasks

Now is the time to check over tools and machinery. Even if the machinery does not get a lot of use, it still needs to be checked and thoroughly cleaned. Not being very mechanically minded, I always take my mower, chainsaw and strimmer to a tool-hire firm for sharpening and servicing. I do not have electric edge-tools such as hedge trimmers, because of the danger of snagging the cable. Even if one uses a power-breaker, which is essential to eliminate the danger of electrocution, it is still an irritating waste of time having to replace the cable in the middle of a job. The shredder also needs stripping down and cleaning, and the blades may need to be removed for sharpening. Nothing is more irritating than not having machinery in good working order when it is needed, and the dark, wintry days ahead are a good time to check up on this.

The mower is, without exception, one of the most difficult pieces of equipment to clean properly, and all sorts of old brushes, from toothbrushes to pan scrubs, have a second life for this purpose. The accumulated dried and caked grass juices can be removed with a damp cloth, and finally all the surfaces wiped over with a slightly oily rag. After knocking skin from my knuckles, and generally getting frustrated as I cursed the design of lawnmowers, I decided that, should I win the national lottery, I would give a high priority to funding the design of one that is hazard-free. I'm sure it would pay handsome dividends.

The tender shrubs have now been wrapped up for winter protection, which has given me a good chance to inspect the plants closely for any disease or insect infestation that may have been overlooked. The pot specimen of the bay laurel (Laurus nobilis) produced a nasty surprise: an infestation of soft scale insect (*Coccus hesperidum*) clearly visible on the underside of the leaves and on the stems.

There is a wide range of scale insects, many of which are specific to certain plants, and their distribution ranges from the tropic to the sub-Arctic areas. The scales are roughly oval, brown in colour, and up to 2 inches long, and they adhere closely to the leaf or stem. They are almost all soft-bodied females, exuding the waxy material that forms the protective scales. They multiply like aphids, parthenogenetically – that is, not necessarily with male help. Since the females may produce anything up to 1,000 crawling nymphs during their three-month life-span, they can be a real problem. The most effective means of control is simply wiping them off the leaves and stems by hand with a soft, soapy rag. Spraying with insecticides is not very successful unless it is carried out before the nymphs form their protective wax scales.

Planning ahead

The last few weeks have seen a variety of seed catalogues arriving through the post, some dealing only with mail orders, others having outlets through garden centres, hardware stores, and so on, as well. I am sure that other gardeners are often as confused as I am by seed catalogues. When I select articles for purchase, I like to be able to shop around for the right prices. But I find it almost impossible to make comparisons because of the difficulty of comparing like with like.

Packet contents are not standardized, and other variations which must affect the cost are selling seeds in foil (except for peas and beans); and the appearance of the packet itself, for some are plain, with minimal instructions and descriptions, while others are enticingly coloured, with pictures and charts for the periods of sowing, flowering and harvesting.

The biggest problem I find is in the multiplicity of new varieties available each year. One well-known supplier lists no less than 14 varieties of garden pea. Most of them are known and tried, and give a range of harvesting right through from mid-June to early October, but there are also five special types, such as mangetout and sugar snap. Another equally famous firm lists only three varieties: one new, one old, and a mange-tout. Since most seeds are produced not by the seed merchants but by specialist growers, I sometimes wonder whether one seed merchant's variety called 'Green Ace' might not be the same as another's 'Autumn Perfection'. We have a seed house in Cumbria which claims to have one of the most extensive seed lists in the country, and as usual at this time of year I get great pleasure from browsing through these, reading up details of plants in one or other of my reference books, and then trying out some of the seeds.

There are many so-called rarities which are really quite easy to grow from seed and are only 'rare' because they are not included in the restricted range available at most garden centres. There are many first-class garden centres throughout the country, but I do on the whole prefer to deal with specialist growers, because they always have a more comprehensive list of the plants they special-ize in. *The Plant Finder* is an excellent publication in which to locate a supplier of plants other than those listed as being widely available.

Plant for the month: *Viscum Album* – Mistletoe

Mistletoe, a slightly sinister parasite, has acquired a disquieting reputation both from Norse legends in which Baldur, the god of peace, was accidentally killed by a mistletoe branch, as well as from association with the mysterious druids to whom, wherever it grew on an oak tree, it was sacred. Used in divination, and cut, only at appropriate phases of the moon, with a golden sickle, mistletoe has never completely shaken off its pagan past and is never used in church decoration, except at York Minster, where, in defiance of all maleficent superstitions, it is traditionally used to decorate the high altar at Christmas.

Flowers for the house

Some restraint through the penitential season of Advent makes the contrast of glittering decoration at Christmas even more effective. Many bare branches arrange well and are easily transformed with a quick spray of silver or gold, and hung with baubles to complement the Christmas tree. Ivy or choisya – Mexican Orange – make glossy dense background greenery, and if you can find a bush of *cotinus coggygria* with a few wine-dark leaves left on the branch, set them where a sun can shine through to create a glow worthy of sunset. The red stems of dogwood are a dramatic support for red carnations.

For small bowls grow winter-flowering pansies, Christmas roses, and short Algerian iris, *unguicularis*. For taller arrangements find winter jasmine, golden mahonia, pink viburnum or twigs of witch hazel, with tiny tufts of vivid gold flowers.

If you are given pot plants as gifts you will wonder, by the end of December, where to put them all.

Flowers for the church

Since Advent covers the first part of December, and the Saints' days and Sunday after Christmas are still white, there is only the preparation for that great festival to consider: but like all celebrations, success is only achieved by careful organization. Several weeks with purple hangings and no flowers ensures the spectacular impact of any church dressed for high festival, and as the first Mass of Christmas is celebrated in the middle of the night, the light of new candles, white flowers, and white vestments is even more impressive.

Greenery needs to be tracked down. The bright green of *Griselinia* is worth considering as a contrast to dark evergreens; holly is a must; as is one heavily berried twig, to be retained for the pudding. Ivy is dirty, but traditional, and in a huge church one might consider pampas plumes as back-up. It is always appreciated if anyone growing white chrysanthemums for the church tells the organizer well in advance. Yew, however tempting, is the tree of life and should be used at Easter. Flowers at this season need to be ordered well ahead, and are expensive.

If the comparatively recent practice of hanging a kissing bough in the centre of the chancel arch, is practised, mistletoe should be replaced by a bunch of ribbons, or a glass bauble, but seven red apples should be hung to reflect the light of four decorative candles.

Many churches decorate a tree for which lights, baubles and a drape for the pot must be found, and an extension lead to the nearest power-point checked.

Finally there is the crib scene, which should include Christmas roses, Madelon's gift to the Christ Child.

December

The children's garden – *Indoor gardening*

Some people prefer to do all their gardening indoors, and there is an enormous range of possibilities. Probably the most obvious is a collection of house plants, arranged to complement each other in a container which would be well placed in a cool hall or garden room.

If you have a cool conservatory you could collect palms – not all of them grow to Kew Garden size – or, if space is limited, a terrarium, that is, an exotic garden growing inside a carboy (large glass container), old fish tank or goldfish bowl. African violets would be a lovely specialization and are easy to propagate from the leaves, or if you enjoy pleasant smells you could try scented-leafed pelargoniums.

Cacti do not require a great deal of time and produce vivid coloured flowers; living stones are somewhat weird, but only need little space; and if you are patient and are attracted by miniatures, bonsai, tiny trees, might appeal to you; or perhaps air plants, which grow on a shell, piece of wood or bark, or you can create a tiny scene with a figure, some pebbles and marbles with one or two air plants.

Best of all might be just one really special plant to care for, a gloxinia, cineraria, or even an orchid.

Get a book from the library and read all about it.

Tailpiece

Over the years we have all become used to having salad stuff – tomatoes, lettuce, spring onions, cucumbers and peppers – at all seasons as a result of easy transport from abroad; our grandchildren listen incredulously to our recollections of the eagerly awaited first tomatoes and lettuce in the shops at a price that our mothers regarded as reasonable, to relieve the monotony of bubble-and-squeak with cold meat and pickle on Mondays. They are surprised, too, at tales of salted runner beans and eggs put into waterglass, a short season for citrus fruits, spinach for most of the year, and no freezer foods. A bygone age indeed, seeming so far away that we wonder if our daughter, when very young, was right when she asked: 'What was it like to ride in a stagecoach, Mummy?'

Things to enjoy

- The diverse patterns of bare trees, especially silhouetted against the winter sky at dawn or sunset.

- Comparing the skeleton designs of deciduous trees with the wonderfully solid shapes of evergreens, particularly during snow or frost.

- Offering hospitality to garden birds.

- Taking time over the Christmas holiday to consider your garden, and planning for next year. Have you enough plants with leaves for flower arranging – hostas, bergenia, various ferns, ivies and periwinkles?

- In wild weather, reading about gardens.

- Satisfaction at the completion of another cycle of seasons, and the expectation of resting with your garden safely stowed away for winter.

- Your increased awareness of all things living at the end of another twelve months in touch with the natural world.